World Geography

World
Industry
& making goods

Atlantic Europe Publishing

CONSTRUCTION CHEMICALS AUTOMOBILES IRON AND STEEL FACTORIES AND THE CITY INDUSTRIAL LOCATION PHARMACEUTICALS

FACTORY HANDMADE CRAFTS WORKSHOPS PRODUCTION LINE WORKING ENVIRONMENT MACHINES ENGINEERING AEROSPACE

How to use this book

There are many ways of using this book. Below you will see how each page is arranged to help you to find information quickly, revise main ideas or look for material in detail. The choice is yours!

On some pages you will find words that have been shown in CAPITALS. There is a full explanation of each of these words in the glossary on page 63.

This heading in the running text tells you about the section that follows.

This is the main column of running text that forms the chapter. Read this for a good understanding of the subject as a whole.

Scan these boxes for key ideas.

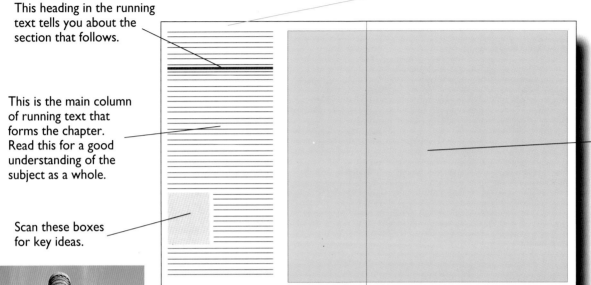

The information in the box describes an important subject in detail and gives additional facts.

Author
Brian Knapp, BSc, PhD
Educational Consultant
Stephen Codrington, BA, DipEd, PhD
Art Director
Duncan McCrae, BSc
Editor
Elizabeth Walker, BA
Illustrator
Simon Tegg
Designed and produced by
EARTHSCAPE EDITIONS
Print consultants
Landmark Production Consultants Ltd
Printed and bound by
Paramount Printing Company Ltd

First published in the United Kingdom in 1995 by Atlantic Europe Publishing Company Limited, 86 Peppard Road, Sonning Common, Reading, Berkshire, RG4 9RP, UK

Copyright © 1995
Atlantic Europe Publishing Company Limited

The Atlantic Europe Publishing logo is a registered trademark of Atlantic Europe Publishing Company Limited.

Suggested cataloguing location

Knapp, Brian
    World Industry & making goods
    – (World Geography; 7)
338

ISBN 1-869860-63-2

Acknowledgements
The publishers would like to thank the following for their help and advice: *Air Reldan Inc.*, New Orleans, Louisiana; *Aspen Flying Club*, Englewood, Colorado; *Bridgeford Flying Service*, Napa, California; *The Royal Commonwealth Society Collection, the Syndics of the Cambridge University Library*, Cambridge, UK; *Eveland Aero*, Honolulu, Hawaii; *David Newell*, Oxfam-Bridge, Thailand; *Honda* (UK); *ICI* (UK); *Paramount Printing Co. Ltd*, Hong Kong; *Rolls-Royce plc* and *Vauxhall Motors Limited* and *Wycombe Aviation*.

Picture credits
(c=centre t=top b=bottom l=left r=right)
All photographs are from the **Earthscape Editions** library except the following: **Honda (UK)** 3br, 53tl, 53tr, 53ctr, 53cbr, 53br; **ICI** 12t, 13cl, 13br, 34cr, 51tr; **Jack Jackson** 9t, 11t, 11b; **Panos Picture Library** 16/17 (Heidi Bradner); courtesy of **Rolls-Royce plc** 1, 2r, 18/19, 33tl, 33tr, 34bl, 35, 45br, 54bl, 54br, 55, 62bl, 63cl, 63bl & FRONT COVER photograph by **Andrew Siddons, Rolls-Royce plc**; by permission of **the Syndics of Cambridge University Library** 23tr, 29br; **The Sutcliffe Gallery** 22b; **UKAEA technology** 54c; **University of Reading, Rural History Centre** 8, 20cl, 21tr, 25t (The Grocer), 26/27, 27tr, 29cr, 43tl; **Vauxhall Motors Limited** 33b, 52/53; **ZEFA** 15tl, 15br, 20bl, 44/45, 46cl, 56/57, 58/59, 61.

This product is manufactured from sustainable managed forests. For every tree cut down at least one more is planted.

Contents

Chapter 1
Facts about industry   5

Companies in change   7
Change, always change   8
Handmade crafts: the beginnings
   of industry   8
Industry and prosperity   10
Workshops: 'factories' on a small scale   10
The many ways of making goods   12
1: Crafts made at home   12
2: Specialised workshops   12
The manufacturing system   12
3: Factories   14
Pride of place for factories?   14
Ever-moving business   14
Industry and environment   17

Chapter 2
Industrial revolutions   19

The first industrial revolutions   20
Goods that were made for survival   20
Machines versus people   22
The importance of crafts and science   22
Transferring ideas around the world   22
The Industrial Revolution   24
The factory is invented   24
Machines of the Industrial Revolution   24
The age of steam power   26
The sites of early factories   26
Mass-production   28
The growth of engineering   28
The scientific revolutions   30
Electricity and changes in factories   30
Automation and robots   32
Industrial and developing worlds   32
Robots, computers and the future   32
The future of manufacturing   34

Chapter 3
Where industries are found   37

Keeping down the cost of supplies   38
Keeping close to markets   38
Where factories are found   38
Land and labour   40
Factories and the city plan   40
Where to find industry in a city   40
The future of factories   42
Parks for factories   42

Chapter 4
A guide to the world's industries   45

Iron and steel   46
Steelworks   46
Iron and steelworks   46
The siting of iron and steelworks   47
The motor vehicle industry   48
Shipbuilding and repairing   48
The chemicals industry   50
Modern automobile making   52
Passenger aircraft   54
Aerospace   54
The electronics industry   56
The computer industry   57
Consumer electronics   58
The textile industry   58
Industrial and military electronics   60
The construction industry   60
Industries of the future   62

Glossary   63

Index   64

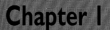

Chapter 1

Facts about industry

Since their invention two centuries ago, factories have changed the world and the way people live. The goods they make give us a world far healthier and more comfortable than we could have had in the past.

But the factories have also had many side-effects which are not altogether desirable. For example, industrialisation has caused people to leave the countryside and create ever-growing congested cities. Industrialisation also means that goods that were once made individually by skilled craftspeople are now mainly mass-produced by people who often have less skill.

Industry – the word people often use when they mean the MANUFACTURING INDUSTRY – in this book means the business of making goods. Goods are such things as bicycles, cups and saucers, computers, washing machines, telephones, clothes. They are the things that help to make our lives comfortable, and they are a vital way that people earn their livings.

❒ Modern manufacturing happens at every scale. Some uses the latest technology and huge capital investment (as shown in this steelworks, left). Much industry, especially in the developing world, uses much simpler equipment (such as the pottery factory, right). But both make goods that we use every day.

People make most of the goods the world needs in special buildings known as FACTORIES. Factories, and the places where many of them are situated – called industrial areas – often make easily recognised parts of any city.

Factories grew up both in the East (first in China) and in the West (first in England) and prospered in the long run because people throughout the world shared their knowledge.

Industries try to take advantage of new discoveries in science and technology. This is why there is constant change.

The word *factory* was in fact taken from a way of working that was first used in India.

Some people would say that without the factory the world's cities would never have grown beyond small centres and we would all still be living in the countryside. And without the success of factories, factory owners would never have had the wealth to pay for many fine city buildings.

Now the world's factories, working alongside its farms and mines, make the majority of the wealth of each country. Where companies have been successful, they now run many factories and employ perhaps hundreds of thousands of workers. The money they make is more than the entire wealth of many countries.

❐ (right) Many new factories use small machines that can be sited in buildings on industrial estates.

On such sites the company rents the building, and when it is no longer suitable they move elsewhere and new tenants take their place. This gives a much more flexible arrangement than when buildings are constructed just for one purpose.

Companies in change

Survival in the world of work is all about change. People who make goods (manufacturers) have the hardest tasks of all. They have to keep their customers supplied with the latest goods. Sometimes, such as with large-scale chemical processes, factories have to be designed around the process that is going on inside. This means that when one process becomes out of date and has to be replaced by another, the building may have to be knocked down or abandoned as well.

Compare that with office work. When computers replaced typewriters, one set of small machines was replaced with another; the building could stay the same.

The enormous cost of change means that large-scale manufacturing is often dominated by huge companies that can most easily cope with the cost of rebuilding.

But a changing world also gives new people with new ideas a chance to succeed. The world's largest companies today are not all the same as those twenty years ago, and it is likely that twenty years from now, many more changes will have occurred.

The world's 25 largest private industrial companies (measured by the value of the goods they sell)
 1. General Motors: motor vehicles (USA)
 2. Royal Dutch Shell: oil and chemicals (Netherlands/UK)
 3. Exxon: oil and chemicals (USA)
 4. Ford: motor vehicles (USA)
 5. Toyota: motor vehicles (Japan)
 6. IBM: computers and business machines (USA)
 7. General Electric: electrical machinery (USA)
 8. British Petroleum: oil and chemicals (UK)
 9. Daimler Benz: motor vehicles (Germany)
10. Mobil: oil and chemicals (USA)
11. Hitachi: electrical and electronic equipment (Japan)
12. Matsushita: electrical and electronic equipment (Japan)
13. Philip Morris: tobacco (USA)
14. Fiat: motor vehicles (Italy)
15. Volkswagen: motor vehicles (Germany)
16. Siemens: electrical and electronic equipment (Germany)
17. Samsung: electronic and electrical equipment (S Korea)
18. Nissan: motor vehicles (Japan)
19. Unilever: soap and food products (UK/Netherlands)
20. El du Pont: chemicals (USA)
21. Texaco: oil and chemicals (USA)
22. Chevron: oil and chemicals (USA)
23. Elf: oil and chemicals (France)
24. Nestlé: food products (Switzerland)
25. Toshiba: electrical and electronic equipment (Japan)

All industries, big and small, help to make wealth, so countries must try to have as much industry as they can. If the number of people making things in a country begins to shrink, chances are that the wealth of the people will begin to slip away.

Change, always change

Industry uses the discoveries of science to make things. This is called technology. So many industries have developed hand in hand with new scientific discoveries.

☞ It was progress in science that allowed the chemicals industry and the automobile to be developed at the end of the last century. One of the world's giant modern industries – computer making – has only been able to grow since scientists invented the silicon chip, the heart of a computer.

> Industries create wealth. Where industries thrive, people become more prosperous.

☞ Factories, and the making of goods using machines, have changed the pace of the world. Factories introduced clocks and the working day; they paced workers to make sure they had done a certain amount of work for their wages.

☞ Factories changed the way people invented things. Before this time goods were modified slowly, and the same design could remain in use for centuries. Factories and the new ways of making goods encouraged people to modify goods often, so that today goods are changed in design, not necessarily because they work any better, but to make more goods for people to buy. In this way factories changed a thrifty world that used goods until they were worn out, then had them repaired, into one which has become used to throwing goods away just to keep in step with new fashion. Now industry has to chase the buying habits of the world.

Handmade crafts: the beginnings of industry

Goods that are made individually by hand are known as crafts. They can be made as part of the household or the handicraft system.

Crafts are one way in which people with modest amounts of money can make goods for sale. In this sense craftwork is attractive to those starting up in business in an industrial country as well as in the DEVELOPING WORLD.

In an industrial country crafts are sought after because they are different to the mass-produced items that we normally buy. In this case, customers realise that they will have to pay extra for the time it has taken for an article to be made by hand, so the skill and imagination of the worker is very important. People who produce simple, uninteresting articles will not succeed.

In the developing world there is some scope for making expensive goods for tourists, but, in general, craftworkers produce more simple items that will sell cheaply on the market. Instead of being items of decoration (as in the industrial world) the crafts made in the developing world are for everyday use.

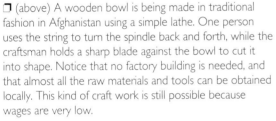

□ (above) A wooden bowl is being made in traditional fashion in Afghanistan using a simple lathe. One person uses the string to turn the spindle back and forth, while the craftsman holds a sharp blade against the bowl to cut it into shape. Notice that no factory building is needed, and that almost all the raw materials and tools can be obtained locally. This kind of craft work is still possible because wages are very low.

□ (right) Using products from the land has always been a way that people could make goods without the cost of paying for raw materials. It allows people with no resources to get on the first stage of making goods to sell. These women from Kenya make colourful baskets in their spare time. Trading companies such as Oxfam then help to ensure that they are marketed worldwide.

□ (left) Hand-crafted chairs, such as this Windsor chair being made in the 1930s, were common and inexpensive in the days before mass-production.

Mass-production has allowed the cost of simple items to stay low, and at the same time allow people to be paid better wages. But because the cost of labour in the industrial world is higher than in the past, custom-made items are now expensive.

Nevertheless, people are getting tired of machine-made items, so there is still a demand for hand-crafting skills. Unfortunately, because skilled work is harder than machine-minding, the number of people wanting to be skilled craftspeople has declined.

Advantages and disadvantages of working at home

The household system is cheap and self-contained. People can make basic goods even if they have very little money, and they can fit in manufacturing tasks among the many other things they have to do each day. But there are many disadvantages: new ideas and new skills are not easily introduced, because there are no master craftspeople or apprentices.

Some household goods can be sold, especially textiles of various kinds. Most household-produced goods, however, are not saleable and do not bring cash to the family.

☛ Factories have also changed as new techniques and new goods are developed. So buildings become unsuited to new machines and have to be renewed, and factory sites become unsuited to new conditions forcing companies to move from one place to another.

Industry and prosperity

Industry can be a fascinating world of traditional ways (handicrafts) and new (modern factories), of small workshops making a few objects a year to giant projects and huge machines, where outputs are measured by millions of tonnes or units.

Large or small, industry can create great excitement and creativity. But although the world of, say, the automobile or the chemical industry, works on a grand scale and is well known, it is important to know that by far the largest number of people work in small businesses. Much of this is a marvellous world of small-scale, careful skilled work, such as in the medical equipment industry.

> Making goods is the cornerstone of prosperity for every country, so developing countries try very hard to get a greater share of the world's manufacturing.

Industry is still the cornerstone of wealth for the world's countries, and there is fierce competition to make the goods that the world's people want to buy. The countries that make the world's goods are mainly the countries that prosper most. In the past these countries were almost entirely in Europe and North America, but today a large part of the world's goods are made by countries in East Asia. It is just another sign of continuing change.

Growth, change and decline of industry are, therefore, all part and parcel of modern life. Change can have good effects on people (when factories need more workers) but it can also spread unhappiness when factories need to shed jobs.

Workshops: 'factories' on a small scale

Workshops have been the cornerstone of many industries, especially those where the finished goods are always specialised and made individually. For example, the jewellery industry is mainly supplied by workshops, each containing perhaps a few tens of people.

Another example is specialised engineering, such as making tools and moulds to be used in other machines. This requires the specialist skills of a lathe worker and every job is different.

Workshops use small buildings and are often family businesses. They make a profit because they keep their costs low, for example by renting cheap buildings in the less attractive parts of a city.

Workshops are not impressive buildings, but they are a vital means of making goods in small amounts and a vital source of skills. The majority of people making goods in the world do so in workshops.

❏ (above) This small industrial estate of workshop units in New Zealand is typical of those found across the industrial world. It allows people to work on a modest scale in purpose-built surroundings. Many units have their own showroom at one end of the building so they can sell directly to their customers.

Skills in workshops
By sharing ideas and enthusiasm, people in a workshop can think through and develop new products much more easily than a person working on their own and often more efficiently than a whole team of consultants in a big factory.
Workshops are good places to train other people – apprentices – who can learn the skills and start up new workshops, and then train other people.

'Putting out' helps workshops

It is not easy for a workshop to make complicated goods containing many parts. Far more space is needed to make and store the components than a single workshop can provide. But it is possible for many workshops each to make some parts and for them to be gathered together and assembled in a final workshop. This system is called putting out; it has been traditionally used in the textile industry as well as in the electrical and engineering industries.

The owner of the goods arranges for the delivery of raw materials to each of the outworkers. They complete a guaranteed amount of work in, say, a week, and then the owner arranges for the finished work to be collected and new materials delivered.

❒ (below and right) Workshops are especially common in the developing world where many people can work in a small area. The picture below shows a *Jeepney* workshop in the Philippines. Notice the lack of large scale machines and mass-production. The picture on the right shows a tailor's shop in India.

The many ways of making goods

People have always needed to make things. From the days when people sharpened sticks to use as hunting spears, materials have been adapted and altered to suit people's needs. However, there are many ways in which goods can be made, from handworking done by a family to the special goods which only a high technology factory can provide. Here are the main ways in which goods are made:

1: Crafts made at home

People can make many of the things they need themselves in their own homes. These include beds, rope, cloth and clothing. However, without special tools, the variety of goods that can be made is quite limited. Quality may also be a problem because people in a household are not likely to have a wide range of skills.

> Factories – special buildings where goods are mass-produced – are at the large-scale end of making goods.

Furthermore, they may not have access to a wide selection of materials.

2: Specialised workshops

Many people realise that they are better off if they specialise, because they will become more skilled in their chosen task. It makes sense, therefore, for those skills to be used for the benefit of everyone.

In many parts of the world the system of specialised handworking has existed for thousands of years. Most people work in small specially-built WORKSHOPS, where the necessary materials and tools can be kept.

Workshops have many advantages. By bringing together people with talent, a workshop can make far more complex goods than people working on their own. Bicycles jewellery, furniture and textiles are all within the range of a workshop.

The manufacturing system

Making goods – manufacturing – needs a lot of organisation. Manufacturers first have to select the RAW MATERIALS that they need to work with. Then they need to build or rent a factory that will house all the machinery. Next they need to organise the machinery inside the factory so that the manufacturing process runs smoothly, and that parts made on one machine are conveniently ready for use on another.

Finally, when the goods are completed they have to be sent to the customer. Sometimes the factory manager will deliver directly, but for items that are mass produced, the goods will most probably be sent to a wholesaler, who will then redirect them to the appropriate shops for sale.

Raw materials or partly finished goods

Transport of materials and finished goods

Supplies of energy, water, etc.

All manufacturing needs supplies of energy. Often the main supply is in the form of electricity produced by a power station. Electricity can be transported easily through power lines, so industries and energy supplies do not have to be sited next to each other.

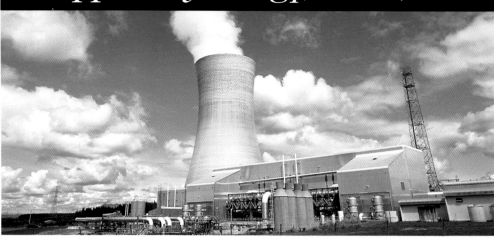

Factory processing

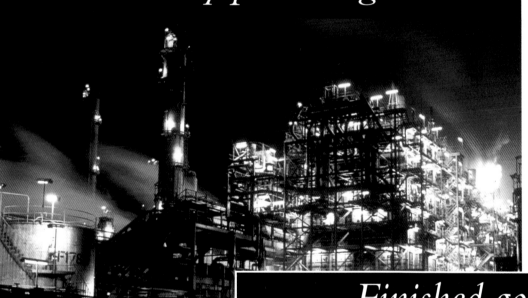

Raw materials are processed inside the factory to make finished products. The nature of the processing will decide the size and shape of the factory site. In this picture the factory is processing very large quantities of chemicals, and so requires a large site.

Finished goods

A small range of raw materials is finally made into a wide range of finished products, each with its own special purpose in the market. These goods have a higher value than the raw materials because of the way the factory has processed them.

Craft and workshops rely on the skills of their workers. Rarely do they have the enormous amounts of money needed to buy large pieces of equipment. This means that, for making goods that need large, expensive machinery or that are cheapest when made on a large scale, it is far more sensible to construct a building for the machinery and to employ the workers in it. For this reason factories were invented.

3: Factories

Factories – special buildings where goods are mass-produced – are at the large-scale end of making goods. They are different to home workers and workshop owners because they invest large amounts of money.

Some factories are almost like giant workshops, because they produce items one at a time. But the key difference is the scale of working and the money that has been invested. The aircraft industry is a good example. Each plane is made up of thousands of items and needs teams of people to construct it. It is complex work using very expensive machinery.

> Most countries still prosper by making goods.

Factories with automated mass-production systems, can concentrate on making all their goods exactly the same. By using fast machinery they can also keep down the time that each item takes to make. The cutlery, iron and steel, chemical, electronics and textile industries are good examples of industries where mass production makes it possible for goods to be manufactured in large quantities and at reasonably low prices.

Pride of place for factories?

Factories and factory owners are responsible for creating the wealth of a country. Many of the original factories were built proudly at the hearts of cities.

Ever-moving business

Of all the goods you see in the shops, chances are that most have been invented in the last few years. As new products are invented, old products are no longer wanted and so go out of production. Factories must continually adapt to the coming and going of their products.

Have you noticed how a new product is always quite pricey, but products that have been on the market longer, and where there is plenty of choice, seem much more reasonably priced? This difference occurs because a new product is unique and some people will pay a high price to be the first to have new goods.

When prices are high, goods can be made almost anywhere – even in cities where costs and wages are high – and still make a profit. But as soon as competitors begin to make similar goods, the price falls. Then producers must move their production lines to the cheapest locations – often in the developing world. This may not be as convenient as places nearer the markets, but it allows the goods to be priced more cheaply and still make a profit.

By the time a product is taken off the market, it may have been made in one factory and then moved three or more times, often finally being made in a completely different country to the one where it was first made. Many electronics goods are like this: they are first made in a factory in, say, the UK, Australia, Japan, Canada or the United States. But when they have to be made more cheaply, the factory moves to a place where costs are lower, say to China or Mexico.

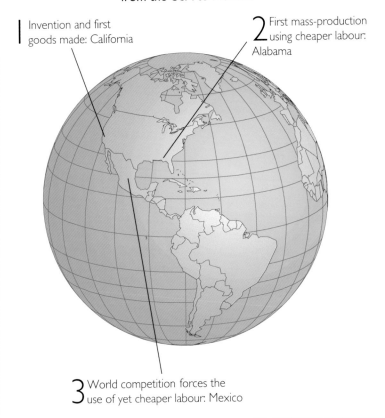

An example of a transfer from the USA to Mexico.

1 Invention and first goods made: California

2 First mass-production using cheaper labour: Alabama

3 World competition forces the use of yet cheaper labour: Mexico

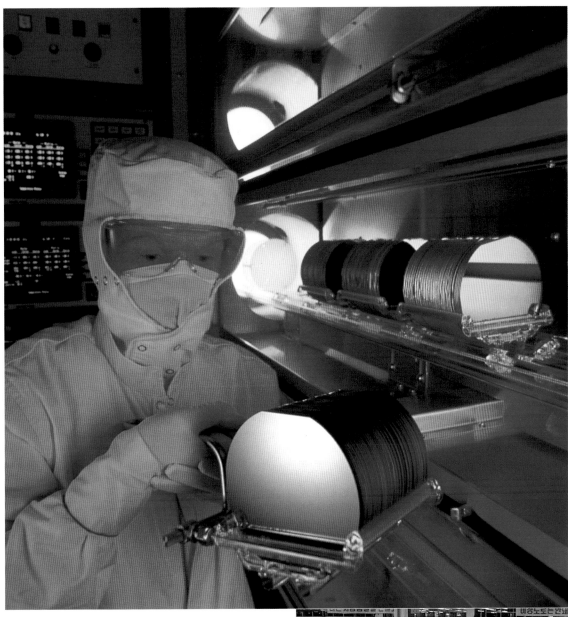

(left) The newest techniques, such as making computer chips, need the most modern machines and the most highly skilled labour. It is therefore still profitable to make such goods in the industrial countries.

An example of a transfer from Japan to China.

1 Invention and first goods made: Japan

2 First mass-production using cheaper labour: Taiwan

3 World competition forces the use of yet cheaper labour: China

(above) Because customers demand the lowest prices for their goods, many products are mass-produced using low-cost labour. This picture shows televisions being assembled using developing world labour.

You might think that factories would be given pride of place in a city and provided with all the best facilities so that they could be successful and bring in more wealth. And yet many planners have now banned factories from their city centres.

Why have city planners have been so apparently ungrateful? One reason is that people in some countries have forgotten that industry brought them their wealth, and they regard industry as nasty, noisy and polluting.

> Industry has to lose its image as a thing which pollutes the environment. Much has been done, but a great deal remains to be achieved.

But, not surprisingly, the loss of factories from many cities has brought higher unemployment and the decay of city centres. Only recently have people in some industrial countries realised that no amount of offices will replace the wealth of a factory.

Many countries in the developing world have had no such worries about their manufacturing, giving it pride of place and making sure that manufacturers get the support they need. In this way they have brought the benefits of industry to their own countries, showing that manufacturing and wealth go hand in hand.

The past that must be dealt with

The future

(above) Modern industries in a landscaped environment need no longer be a cause for environmental concern.

Industry and environment

Many of the processes that were used during the early stages of the industrial revolution were primitive, wasteful of materials and caused enormous amounts of pollution. At the same time, there was much less concern for the effects of industry on the environment than there is today.

Many industries, especially companies that work on a large scale, have now found ways of being far less wasteful of raw materials and far less polluting. For example, for every tree used to make books like the one you are reading, at least another tree is planted in its place, and far less harmful bleach is used to make the paper white than was used in the past.

❏ (left) East European communist legacy. A woman factory worker demonstrates the amount of pollution that settles on the nearby landscape. The source is the steelworks in the background which still uses old, inefficient equipment. The industries of Eastern Europe represent one of the biggest environmental challenges facing the world.

Chapter 2

Industrial revolutions

We live in an age where new goods appear on the shelves of shops every day. We are used to new replacing the old, but how often do we think about how goods are made and ask: What is happening behind the scenes? How are these things made and what causes people to invent new things? When we do, we find a rich tradition of invention across the world.

In every part of the world, centres of invention have thrived and moved from place to place during the centuries. In the past, inventions were centred in the Middle East, India and China. For the last hundred years or so much invention appears to have come from Europe, North America and Japan. In the future we can expect the centres of invention to be more evenly spread throughout the world; already countries like China and Korea have gained the knowledge to compete with Japan, just as Japan learned to compete with Europe and America.

In the past, opportunities for making new things occurred everywhere, but blossomed best where there was a stable society. This gave time for inventions to be tested and developed. In societies constantly at war, very little progress

❐ (left) The robot revolution is coming to many of the large mass-production factories, like this one run by Rolls-Royce. As robots are made to perform more intelligent tasks, factory space can be designed around them and productivity can be made higher still.

As the most repetitive tasks are taken over by robots, people are free to do more creative jobs. To fit in with the newest revolution, however, people have to be prepared to be retrained and to develop more skills, or finding a job may be more difficult.

was made. This was why China, stable for thousands of years, was the centre of so much invention.

The first industrial revolutions

The INDUSTRIAL REVOLUTION (that is, the one many people learn about in their history books) began in Great Britain in the 18th century. Yet this Industrial Revolution was really one important step in a series, each step being more impressive than the one before.

The first step on the road to modern industry occurred tens of thousands of years ago when people discovered they could make arrow heads and axe heads by chipping certain types of stone, like flint. This time is now called the Stone Age.

The next step happened more than three-thousand years ago, when people discovered that metals could be extracted from rock by heating it. The metal could then be refashioned into useful objects, such as farming tools, like hoes, and weapons, like swords. This period, when the metals extracted were mainly copper and tin, is called the Bronze Age. It was followed about a thousand years later by the discovery of how to make furnaces hot enough to extract iron from rocks. This is known as the Iron Age.

> Early industry was driven by the need for food and clothes, and for weapons for war.

Metals were worked and the techniques were developed quite separately in various parts of the world. However, early ways of metal working could not produce good quality metal, and this limited the usefulness of the things people could make. For example, in northern China bells and ploughs were made from cast iron, a very brittle material that would never be used for such purposes today. Nevertheless, in China, as early as the 11th century, over 125,000 tonnes of iron were being made each year.

Goods that were made for survival

Goods are often very practical things, made to make life easier for people. Farming is such a basic part of human survival, and such hard work that many of the first inventions and the earliest machines were often designed to make farming a little less backbreaking. For example, the Chinese began to irrigate their land because the growth in population meant they had to grow more and more food. They invented the plough to cultivate the ground more quickly, and the wheel was used as a pulley for drawing water.

Clothing has also been needed since earliest times, and machines were eventually made to speed up the making of cloth.

People have also always needed to be able to protect themselves. It is no use being skilled at farming and cloth-making if you are captured by a more warlike people. So the making of weapons was always an important task. It led to inventions in metalworking, which in turn provided the iron that allowed farm tools and machines to be improved.

So the need to survive produced three closely related industries over a thousand years ago: farming, textiles and metalworking. Today, the world around us may seem very remote from this ancient world, but in reality little has changed. The world is still driven by a need for food, clothing and defence.

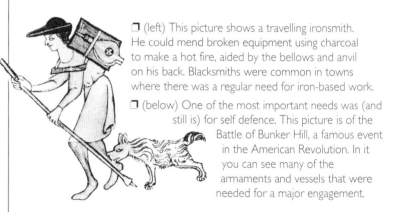

❐ (left) This picture shows a travelling ironsmith. He could mend broken equipment using charcoal to make a hot fire, aided by the bellows and anvil on his back. Blacksmiths were common in towns where there was a regular need for iron-based work.

❐ (below) One of the most important needs was (and still is) for self defence. This picture is of the Battle of Bunker Hill, a famous event in the American Revolution. In it you can see many of the armaments and vessels that were needed for a major engagement.

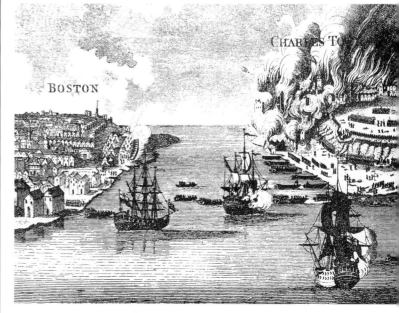

❐ (above) The wheelwright (wheel-maker) was one of the most important people making goods before the Industrial Revolution, because the horse and wooden cart were essential to trade.

Wheel-making for farm vehicles continued right through the Industrial Revolution and is still carried on today. This picture dates from the 1950s. It shows that true craft skills cannot readily be replaced by machines.

❐ (right) Clothes have been made by simple traditional techniques for thousands of years. This is a Mexican hand-weaving frame

To get the iron hot enough to melt, great blasts of air were sent over coals using huge bellows driven by oxen, water wheels or people. Thus, the need to improve this one material, iron, led to a range of related inventions (such as the blast furnace and the machinery of the bellows).

Machines versus people

In many countries, such as India, there seemed little point in developing machines other than for special uses. India had a large number of people, and it was, at that time, more efficient for people to do the tasks than to spend time and effort making machines that did not really do the job any better. (There are many examples from all over the world where using people instead of machines still makes sense even today.)

Industry thrived wherever governments supported it.

But where there were fewer people (such as in Europe) and harder tasks (such as ploughing the hard soils of China), people tried to make machines.

The importance of crafts and science

Making ploughshares and swords are quite simple engineering tasks. The importance of craftspeople is that they do not just make simple things; rather, they test out the limits of a material and their skills to make very fine products. A country that has a long tradition of skilled work is more likely to be able to make complicated goods when they are required.

Science is important in a similar way. Science encourages people to collect facts from experiments and then to analyse them. In this way experiments with the atmosphere led to an understanding of how gases behave, which in turn led to the development of the steam engine and the internal combustion engine.

Transferring ideas around the world

It is rare that people can develop products on their own. Instead, ideas usually develop much faster when people work as a group. Each person is stimulated by ideas from others in the group. In the same way, one country rarely develops ideas on its own; sooner or later, people come into contact with new ideas from other countries and take them home.

These transfers of technology have been extremely important in the development of world industry. For example, the Indians and Chinese learned from each other by regular trading contact. The Islamic world and the Indians also traded, so that eventually Islamic and Chinese ideas were shared. Through trade and visits, the technology of Islamic countries was eventually transferred to Europe, especially mechanical clocks and gunpowder.

The medieval world had three great mechanically minded centres: China, the Islamic countries and Europe. Europe was especially well placed to take advantage of the new knowledge because it was developing a skilled workforce to make the ploughs and other farm equipment it needed. It quickly developed the mechanical clock and the cannon, and, soon after, guns. Guns had to be made from the highest quality metals, and with great precision. Warfare drove many inventions, just as it does today.

❐ (below) As trade flourished, people were able to see for the first time the goods made in other parts of the world. As ships travelled from port to port, their designs were copied and improved on. In this way ships worldwide became more similar.

☐ (above) Migration and colonisation caused many skills to be transferred around the world. This simple historic boat found on a lakeside in Canada shows all the skills of its immigrant Irish builders.

☐ (above) Tools that people made varied enormously with the lifestyle of the people. The Plains Indians of North America, for example, made their homes of timber and buffalo skins. There was little transfer of technology, simply because they felt no need for added material goods. Thus, they did not adopt the wheel and continued to use sledges for transport. As a result their lifestyle changed little even though they had contact with outsiders for centuries. In the end, though, the conflict in lifestyles became so great that it resulted in wars.

Firearms

The first people to make firearms were the Chinese. They invented gunpowder and used it to frighten away attackers. They also made the earliest cannons.

During the 14th century this technology became known in war-torn Europe. It caused great excitement, because those who could make firearms most effectively would have an enormous advantage over those still using swords.

Early guns were made with barrels made of iron strips fastened together with iron hoops or of cast brass or bronze. Later, guns used iron castings. It was the bell-making foundries that soon learned how to cast cannon barrels and later musket and handgun barrels. But casting left rough barrels that had to be filed smooth by hand. The gunsmith thus became an important craftsman.

The new technology in weapon-making put an end to castle-building and made people turn instead to forts. Forts were built in a star shape which would help deflect cannon balls. Forts were also designed to have cannons on their walls and places for musketeers to fire from.

Cannons were soon added to ships, leading to the famous galleons which had guns on both flanks showing through special gun ports.

The scientific *method* of experimenting and analysing was also the vital key that set people thinking about how to improve, or invent, a whole range of machines that could make work faster and easier.

The Industrial Revolution

The worldwide problem for manufacturers in the 18th century was how to keep the price of goods down. Because goods were all made by hand, low prices could only be achieved by keeping down the total wage bill.

Asia, Europe and North America responded differently to this problem. Asia turned to better farming, growing more food and thus keeping down food prices. With low food prices it was also possible to pay low wages. In Europe, though, the harsher climate and soils meant that food costs, and thus wages, stayed high. This meant that employers were keen to find ways of getting more for their money.

> Employers were keen to find ways of getting more for their money – and this meant using more machines.

This led Europe – and especially Britain – to take the lead in the Industrial Revolution. In iron-making, it was Abraham Darby in Coalbrookdale, England, who independently developed the use of coal (in the form of coke) for blast furnaces to increase the output of his furnaces. Thus, Europe and then North America turned into the workhouse of the world, leaving Asia behind for nearly two centuries.

The factory is invented

There was one further problem in reducing costs: a great shortage of skilled people to make goods. Manufacturers began looking around to find ways of using less-skilled people. They noticed, for example, how armies turned unskilled people by careful

Machines of the Industrial Revolution

The Industrial Revolution replaced skilled people with less skilled machine minders. The minders had to keep up with the speed of the machines, and therefore the speed of output could be guaranteed. This was the real basis of the Industrial Revolution.

People were also fascinated by clocks, not just because they were mechanical marvels, but also because they allowed people to become more organised. With the widespread use of clocks came a new way of life, where everyone worked certain hours, leading to the invention of the working day. This was an essential change in allowing people to synchronise their activities.

Because each machine only did part of a complete task, it was important that all the machines were gathered in a special-purpose building. Then the output of one machine could be fed directly to the next. The special buildings in which the new working system and its machines were housed became known as the *factory*.

❐ (below and below far right) This building houses one of the world's early steam engines, fuelled by coal. It is a huge beam engine. One arm of the beam extends out of the building and is connected to a wheel. As the beam rocks up and down, it turns the wheel, causing a pump to work in a shaft underground. This pump was used to drain water from mine shafts. Engines of this kind made the Industrial Revolution possible.

Steam engines were also used to turn drive shafts. Engine houses such as these were always found alongside factories and it was their smokestack chimneys that gave the industrial landscape of the 19th century its most distinctive look (see page 27).

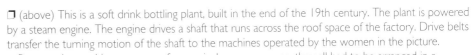
(above) This is a soft drink bottling plant, built in the end of the 19th century. The plant is powered by a steam engine. The engine drives a shaft that runs across the roof space of the factory. Drive belts transfer the turning motion of the shaft to the machines operated by the women in the picture.

Because the machines were run from a single power source, they all had to be arranged in a purpose-built factory.

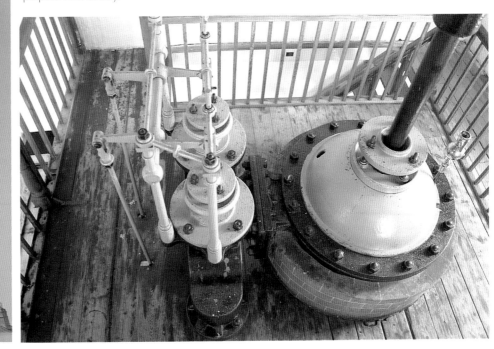

training and organisation into 'fighting machines', with each person treated as part of a giant machine to be organised as a whole.

Manufacturers started to look at how the scarce skilled worker could be replaced with people who were less skilled.

The answer was to look at what the skilled worker did, divide it up into separate (and therefore simpler) tasks, and try to have less-skilled people mind machines that would do each of the simpler tasks.

In the 18th century, the trading posts owned by the British East Indian Company were run by agents, called *factors*. Their job was to order goods from Indian workers and also to supervise, or manage, the speed at which the goods arrived in the company's warehouse for shipment to England. This system, combined with the idea of replacing skilled workers with less-skilled workers, produced the idea of the *factory*, a place where goods were made by a chain of less-skilled workers who were organised and supervised by managers.

> The factory was a place where goods were made by a chain of low-skill workers who were organised and supervised by managers.

The age of steam power

The earliest factories were built by the textile industry, and had machines made from wood and operated by water power. On their own, water-powered wooden machines were no different in principle to the mills that had been around for thousands of years. What made the difference was the use of steam power and metal machines.

The Industrial Revolution was due to three things:

- ☞ the use of machines made of iron;
- ☞ the use of people as machine minders; and
- ☞ the use of power to drive the machines

The sites of early factories

The world's first factory was built in the countryside in Derby, England, in 1702. One of the machines used in it was for unreeling silk from cocoons.

The first factories, like the one in Derby, were powered by water, so they had to be close to fast-flowing streams. But these streams are nearly always found in steep-sided valleys, forcing the factories to build in cramped sites. In addition, direct water power can only drive a limited number of machines, so factories were limited in their growth.

All this changed with the invention of the steam engine. The need to fuel the steam boiler with coal meant that the overwhelming priority was to be close to a coal mine, or at least near a canal so that coal could be brought by barges. Coal was a much more concentrated source of energy, so factories began to grow bigger. They crowded together on the coal mines, and by canals and railway lines, to become the world's first industrial cities.

❐ (right) Halifax, England, one of the world's earliest factory centres. Although the tall boiler chimneys have now gone, the splendid factory buildings remain.

❐ (below) A factory in the city of Bristol, England, as it was seen in the 19th century. Bristol, being a port, was in a good communications position. By good fortune it was also sited near a coalfield, so it was able to take advantage of steam power and attract many industries.

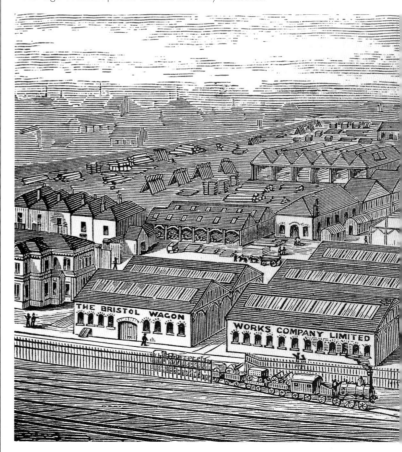

❐ (below) As the age of steam progressed and steam trains were able to carry coal away from the coal fields, some factories grew up away from the traditional cities. New 'green-field' sites suited engineering companies because they used limited amounts of coal. Those, like iron and steel factories, that used vast amounts of raw materials remained firmly tied to the coal and iron fields.

Some green-field factories were built in isolated towns and villages. Perhaps the owner had started a small workshop in his home town and then simply built bigger and bigger works at the same site. Sometimes a city even grew up around them.

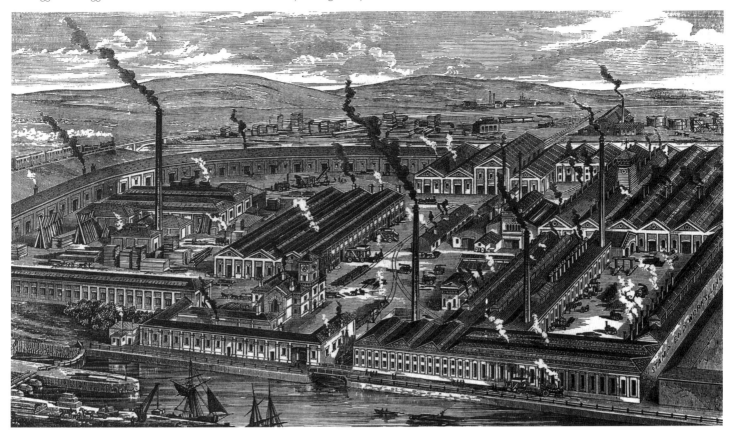

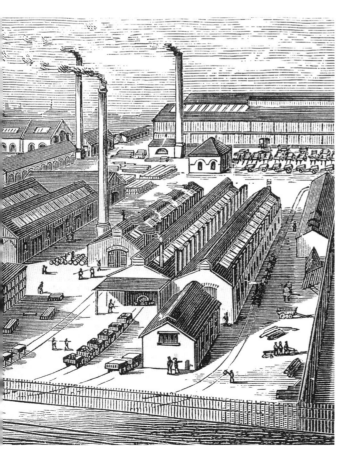

❐ (above) Bliss Mill, England, was a textile mill built in the countryside. It was sited near to the traditional raw material (wool from the nearby farmland sheep). Coal was brought to the site. This beautiful industrial building was constructed to be a factory and also to show the wealth and pride of the owner. Like all steam-powered factories, it had many stories, each powered by drive shafts from the same boiler.

The first steam engine was invented in England in 1699 by Thomas Savery, and was used to pump water from coal mines. It was a very inefficient engine and a fearsome consumer of coal. But it was far better than anything else, so it was immediately in demand. The steam engine was developed by James Watt in the 1780s and in a short time was used to power machines.

Steam power allowed machines to do far more than was possible previously.

Soon new uses were found for the steam engines, including pumping air into blast furnaces. The new source of power allowed machines to become bigger, and to be faster and more powerful. It allowed factories to become independent of the streams that had previously powered their water wheels, and instead they moved to the coal fields whose coal powered their engines.

In this way coal mining, steam engines and iron-making prospered together, creating a new 'heavy' industry that gave wealth to Europe and North America for nearly two centuries.

Mass-production

The need for weapons in the 19th century, in particular for the Civil War in the United States, caused the next great change in industrial methods and eventually led to the modern way of making things.

The United States government wanted to make guns with *interchangeable parts,* so that they could be repaired quickly on the battlefield. This new idea would also make factory *assembly* of guns faster, and therefore cheaper. To achieve this the old methods of hand finishing guns had to be replaced by new *machine tools* that could make shapes far more accurately than had ever before been thought possible.

The growth of engineering

One vital element was missing from the Industrial Revolution at the turn of the 19th century – easy and cheap transport to get goods to their customers. Canals were expensive to dig, so a dense network of canals was impossible. But the invention of the steam railroad provided the answer.

The first railway in the world was in England. It ran between Darlington (on a coalfield) and Stockton (on the nearby Tees river), and it was designed to carry coal to the coast for export. A year later the world's first passenger railroad opened to carry people between the English cities of Liverpool and Manchester.

Railways needed vast amounts of iron (and later steel) for their rails and locomotives. Great demands were placed on the iron and steel industries by the railway industry, along with pressures from the textile industry. Metal workers quickly developed great skills, and they formed the basis of the engineering industry, the fastest growing industry of the 19th century.

❐ (above) Factory-owners of the Industrial Revolution were often wealthy enough to be important in local government and have a hand in city planning. Here some of these 'city fathers' are remembered in a memorial sculpture, Birmingham, England.

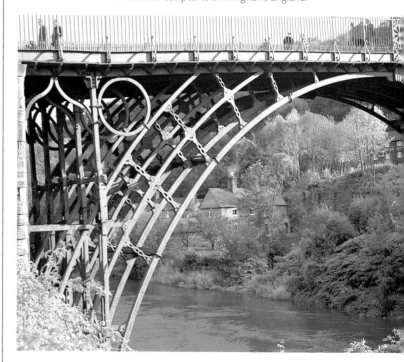

❏ (above) The inside of an engineering works was very different at the end of the 19th century than it is today. Most processes were still done by hand: pieces were cast into sand moulds and then finished by hand. It could be done only because labour was cheap. The inefficiency of this process caused Henry Ford to develop a mass-production line, therefore changing the nature of industry for ever.

❏ (left) The world's first iron bridge was built in England in 1778 near the Abraham Darby ironworks, the first ever to use coal.

❏ (above) The growth of railways gave a tremendous boost to metal industries because of the huge amount of rail track, engines and rolling stock needed. Much equipment was sent to colonies such as Sri Lanka, shown above. At the same time the train allowed manufactured goods to be shipped more cheaply and so allowed prices to fall, which in turn allowed more goods to be bought.

Better accuracy meant that the factory system could now be used in the engineering industry, where before all parts had been made by hand in workshops.

Standardised parts soon became the rule. They allowed what is known as the mass-production method of manufacturing. This, in turn, was the basis for the *production line* system developed by Henry Ford for his motor cars in the 1920s.

The scientific revolutions

The first Western industrial revolutions were *mechanical* revolutions: they depended on machines made by engineers. New revolutions depend on scientific discoveries in both physics (electricity) and chemistry (materials).

Chemists first discovered how to remove impurities from steel and to combine metals to make alloys. They developed filaments for light bulbs and ways of making dyes from factory-made chemicals.

> Henry Ford pioneered the use of the production line in making cars. This form of mass-production allowed goods to be made very quickly and efficiently.

These new industrial revolutions happened fastest where science could most easily be studied: France, Britain, Germany and the United States. Many famous modern German businesses (Bayer, Hoeschst, BASF) were founded by chemists. From this time on, factories could not simply be places where things were made; they had to have *laboratories* where new products could be *researched*.

Perhaps the most important success of the chemists in this period was the discovery of a whole range of materials that used oil or coal as their raw materials. These 'organic chemicals' include all the plastics that are so common in our lives today.

Electricity and changes in factories

Science discovered many entirely new properties and products. Among the most important of these were the electric motor (which could be made in much smaller sizes than a steam engine), the internal combustion (car) engine (which, by using petroleum, could be made smaller and more portable than a steam engine), and the diesel engine, which uses petroleum much more efficiently.

Each of these inventions was important in changing the nature of factories and factory life.

The steam-driven factory
The coal-fired steam boiler ran at a constant speed and was controlled by slipping the drive belts on and off the drive shaft. The need for all machines to work off the same drive shafts controlled the shape of the factory, keeping it compact, with many floors.

A lack of powered transport also meant that people used gravity to move goods wherever possible. Old factories were, therefore, arranged so that the raw materials were hauled to the top floor of the factory. Then, as processing went on, the goods were transferred from machine to machine in such a way that they ended up as finished goods on the ground floor, where they could be shipped to customers.

❒ (below) The image of the factory of the past: small-scale and poorly built. Some less profitable companies still operate in such environments, but most have changed and the old buildings have been demolished or turned into museums.

The electrically powered factory

The big advantages of the electric motor are that it can be controlled very precisely and can be made very powerful. These two advantages changed the nature of the factory completely. For example, the precise control of a motor car assembly line could never have been possible in the age of steam.

Because each machine is powered separately, the layout of the modern factory can be planned for the best efficiency of the work. Electric powered robots can carry goods around the factory. As a result factories are more spacious and can be built on a single level.

◻ (above) Factories, such as this brewery, are now often built so that they blend into the landscape.

◻ (above) The flatted-factory of Asian cities is one of the few places where you can find multistorey modern factories. This simply reflects the shortage of space in the cities.

Inside, each floor works as an independent unit. Goods are moved up and down between floors using electric lifts.

Automation and robots

Electronics, making products that use the properties of electricity, had been developed at the beginning of the 20th century. Both radio and television were being made in new-style factories, using people trained in new skills. And as World War II got under way in 1939, people were beginning to build the first computer.

The computer has altered everyone's life. It has created a whole new industry where none existed before, and it has allowed machines to be guided and factories to be automated in ways that no-one thought possible.

The most recent revolution has been making goods entirely by machine. This is the Robot Age.

Of course this has brought change – yet another industrial revolution. A wide range of labour-saving changes has allowed more goods to be produced using fewer people. Computers and automation (including the use of robots) have caused more jobs to be shed from the factory system than at any previous time in the history of the factory. And it has been the computer that has made the need for teaching people new skills more urgent than ever before.

Industrial and developing worlds

The scientific revolutions opened a gap between the parts of the world that had become industrialised (Europe, North America, Australasia) – which are now called the industrial world – and those countries where handicrafts and farming were still the main ways of earning a living. These became known as the developing world.

Japan was already an industrial power in the 19th century. It had traded fine steel swords with the West for centuries, and it was anxious

Robots, computers and the future

The world of factories that began by using people as machines in the 18th century has now moved on. In most modern factories, simple tasks can be done more efficiently by robots than by people. It is not simply a matter of speed: the machines work more precisely, with fewer faults.

The next stage of manufacturing uses computers to design parts, make them and then fit them together. This is called Computer Integrated Manufacturing (CIM).

By using robots, parts can be made that fit better and last longer than in the past. Robots have a further advantage; because they are controlled by computers, robots can be given new tasks very quickly, simply by changing the computer program. When people are used, they have to be retrained for new tasks.

Interestingly, robots are making factories smaller. Because the robot is so flexible it can make a small number of one product and then switch to making another. This is what allows factories to produce smaller numbers of products than in the past, thus matching customer demands for a wider range of products at a low cost.

1946–65

Beginnings of new industries based on new technology (televisions, start of computers, etc.).

Production first on a small scale, with little automation.

Customers expect to replace their goods after a short time.

Price of goods not very important.

Result: Growth in employment and prosperity.

1965–70

Start of increasing scale of production.

Factories concentrate on more efficient ways of making goods.

Result: Market still growing but fewer new jobs.

1970 to present

Very large firms appear, the results of takeovers.

Customers become more concerned with price and value for money, so even more efficient ways of making goods are sought.

Some processing moved to the developing world to cut wage costs.

Some more automation of basic processes, but the era of mass-production comes to an end as customers want more choice and variety. Workers need to be more skilled.

Customers are now mainly replacing old worn-out goods.

Result: Factories are so efficient they can produce more than customers need. The numbers without jobs increase and only those with skills find it easy to get a job.

❐ (above) This chart shows that in just over half a century industry has changed considerably.

❒ (below) Demand for highly skilled workers has never been higher, but the need for unskilled people has fallen.

❒ (right and below) The factory floor for mass-produced items has changed considerably. Many products are made by machine to higher standards and better quality than people can manage.

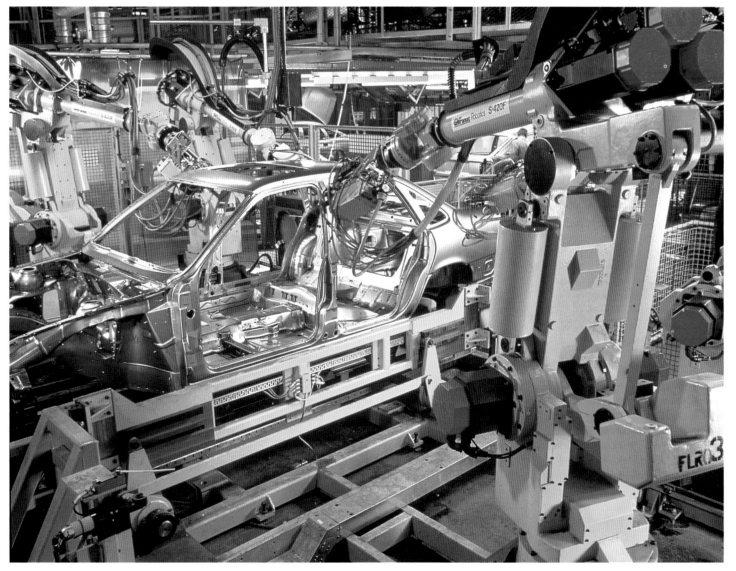

to keep up with modern ideas. Much of its development was in weapons, but it also brought in new industries, such as a railway system from Britain.

Japan chose to remain isolated, however. Until World War 2, Japan's industry mainly concentrated on making weapons, producing many useful skills and good engineers. This is why after World War 2 the Japanese were able to use these skills for more peaceful uses. This time is called the economic miracle, and it quickly made Japan into a world leader for industry.

As more and more developing countries become industrial, prosperity from factories is spreading round the world.

Other countries took longer to industrialise, in many cases because they remained colonies and not independent countries. But, especially in East Asia, they are catching up fast. China has been a 'sleeping giant' for over a century; its people suffered many wars and revolutions, all of which held back progress. China has the world's largest population and its people have a long tradition of careful skilled work. Now China is beginning its own industrial miracle, doubling every five years the volume of goods made in its factories.

❐ (above) New high technology requires far more research and planning than was needed for the simple goods made in the past. Thus the balance of workers changes, fewer being needed on the shop floor and more in the factory offices.

The future of manufacturing

There continues to be a revolution in the way industry works. The giant factories of just a few years ago, producing the same goods for everyone worldwide, are now increasingly rare. As customers continue to demand a wider range of products, it will become even more difficult to make goods in very high volumes, and large companies are already splitting up their work into smaller units, each geared to a different part of the market.

In the future, robots will be able to guide other robots to work a mass-production system, so that even more unskilled jobs will be lost, while the need for scientists and technologists will grow.

❐ (below) Research and development continue to be the foundation for success in industry. The laboratory is already as important as the shop floor. In the future, people who have high qualifications and skills will find jobs easily.

❐ (below) In industries where large amounts of labour are still required, goods will be made in factories in countries where labour costs are low. Most of these will be in Asia.

Chapter 3

Where industries are found

Goods are made all over the world in buildings of all shapes and sizes. But wherever people make goods, they always try to choose a place that will be convenient for their workers, for receiving materials and energy and for sending out finished goods.

Factories provide jobs for many people throughout the world and have a central part in our lives. Yet chances are there is not a factory close to where you live. This may seem all the more strange when you remember that many cities grew up to house workers for factories.

There are many reasons why this should be so, and they make up the story of this chapter. But the reasons are easiest to understand when you remember that factories and industrial cities have been around for two centuries, and that what might once have been a convenient and desirable place for a factory in the past may not be so useful today.

❐ (left) Finding a site for this large business was not easy. It needs an enormous amount of flat land to set out its various pieces of equipment. Its goods must come and go by ship and rail, and its workforce needs to be able to live reasonably close by.

The site that has been found is an estuary, a marshy area of land next to a river but close to the sea. The remaining marsh can be seen in the background. Like most factories, therefore, this business has found a site near to a navigable river.

Keeping down the cost of supplies

Factories need supplies of materials, people and energy to make the goods they sell. Supplies are often bulky and heavy and they are expensive to carry. So the more it costs to carry the supplies to the factory, the more important it is to try to be close to where they are obtained: the ground, if they are minerals, or the factory that produces them, if they are part-finished goods.

> In the 19th century, the need for cheap coal supplies meant that industrial cities developed around coalfields.

Of course finding a suitable site gets more complicated if the factory needs several different supplies. But a compromise can nearly always be found.

In the 19th century, before electricity was discovered, the most expensive supply of all was coal. Coal powered the boilers that produced the steam that ran the machines. But making steam from coal is not very efficient, so huge amounts of coal were needed. This is the reason most of the industrial cities of the 19th century grew up on coal fields.

Keeping close to markets

The cost of taking the finished factory goods to market can also be important. For example, if the finished goods are more fragile (as for glass), more bulky (as in foamed board) or more perishable (as in processed foods) then it may be vital to be near to where the goods are sold. Flour, for example, is easy to transport in bulk, but when it has been made into bread it is bulky, will crush and can go stale within hours of being baked if handled carelessly.

However, trucks, railways, pipelines and ships have become faster and cheaper, and electricity is easy to transport to wherever it is needed, so being close to a market or to supplies is not as important as it used to be.

Where factories are found

Factories are found where the owners feel they can be most profitable. Here are some of the places where they are commonly seen. Of these, a site near a source of raw materials is the least likely today, although in the 19th century one raw material – coal – drew most of the world's industry to places where it was mined.

At a place where raw materials are found

8 Where there is flat land to put a large factory unit or to store raw materials

7 At a meeting point of routes

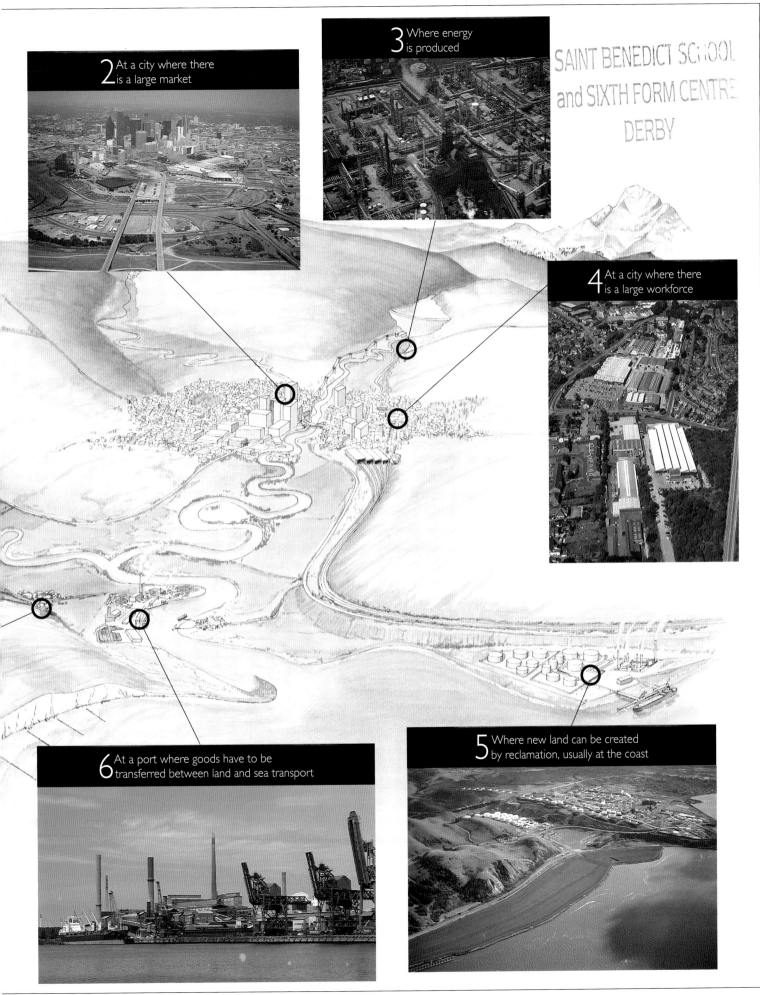

2 At a city where there is a large market

3 Where energy is produced

4 At a city where there is a large workforce

6 At a port where goods have to be transferred between land and sea transport

5 Where new land can be created by reclamation, usually at the coast

For this reason, many factories that were once tied to their supplies of raw material and energy have been able to move to new sites.

Land and labour

Many factories share the same kind of raw materials, and so they may all tend to be sited in the same place. In general, the more people who want to use the same piece of land, the more the successful buyer has to pay. Factories use up large amounts of land and cannot afford to pay as much as those who want to build offices and homes.

For this reason factories tend to be in parts of a city that others don't want, such as on land near rivers that might flood, near docks or in the noisy areas beside major highways.

In the past, cost of transport often decided where a factory would be built; today it is often decided by the cost of land and workers.

City governments make life even harder for many businesses by insisting that factories can only be built in certain parts of a city. These are often called industrial estates.

Wages are usually much the same within a country, so factories may not be too influenced by wage costs inside a country; but wages in the developing world are very much lower than those in industrial countries. This is why, over the last few years, more and more factories have been built in the developing world.

Factories and the city plan

You can see that it is not easy to choose the best place to operate a business because there are so many things to consider. So how is it that so many industries become grouped together rather than scattered across a country?

One reason is that many businesses cannot afford to construct their own buildings. They have to rent a building from a property company.

Land near rivers is often flat and makes good industrial sites.

Where to find industry in a city

Look around any city and you will find industry scattered around. But look closer and you will find that the places where factories are sited actually follow some basic rules. These are shown on this page.

To find out what modern industry needs, look at where the modern factories are located. To see which sites are no longer suitable look at where factories are for let or sale or where they appear abandoned. Page 30 explains why modern factories do not want to be in the same place as some older factories.

Factories also have to compete with other users, such as offices, for land. In general, people building office blocks can afford to pay more for the land than factory owners, especially in city centres, so few factories will be found there.

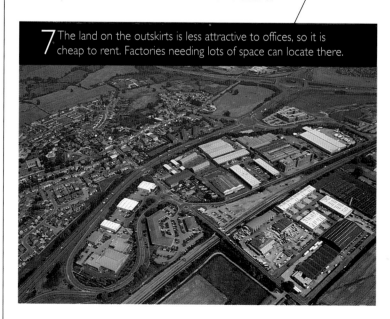

7 The land on the outskirts is less attractive to offices, so it is cheap to rent. Factories needing lots of space can locate there.

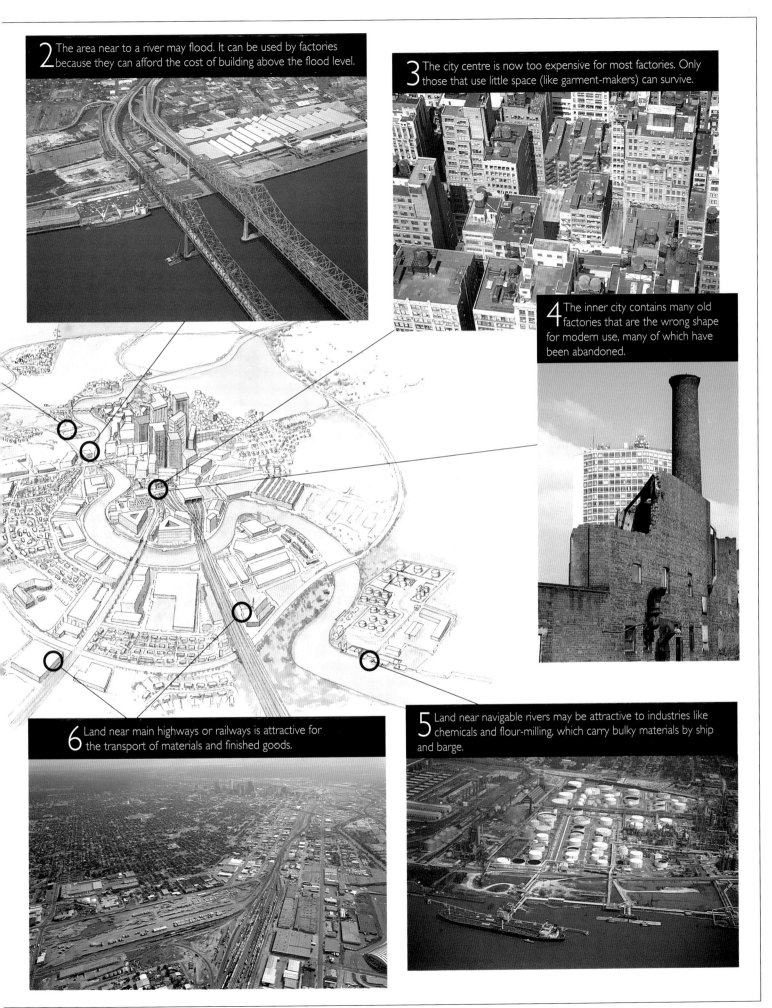

2 The area near to a river may flood. It can be used by factories because they can afford the cost of building above the flood level.

3 The city centre is now too expensive for most factories. Only those that use little space (like garment-makers) can survive.

4 The inner city contains many old factories that are the wrong shape for modern use, many of which have been abandoned.

6 Land near main highways or railways is attractive for the transport of materials and finished goods.

5 Land near navigable rivers may be attractive to industries like chemicals and flour-milling, which carry bulky materials by ship and barge.

Property companies make better profits if they can put up many buildings on a site, so they are in favour of developing industrial estates. Most small businesses, and even some large ones, are now found on industrial estates. Some industrial estates are built to serve special types of industry, which can be seen in their names. They may be called business parks (which really means offices), science parks (which means research and development) or industrial parks (which means manufacturing).

City planners also have a large say in the siting of factories. They want to keep noise and pollution away from homes, so they tend to zone industry to special parts of the city.

> With their landscaped grounds, factories now fit better in a city, and people worry less about living near them.

The future for factories

If you had been living a hundred years ago you could hardly have guessed how factories would change. So how might factories change in the future?

Already the giant factories of the past are being split up into separate businesses and replaced by smaller factories. This is why you see far fewer giant factories today, and also why you see the factories of famous companies scattered in many cities and countries, rather than in just one large site.

In the past, the idea was to make huge amounts of the same goods. But people are now much more fussy about what they want, so goods are made with more variety but in smaller amounts.

Factories are far less polluting than they were, and pressure from customers will make sure they become even more careful with the environment. They will be in attractive landscaped grounds. Soon, planners may even feel that they can be placed among the houses once more, this time in the suburbs.

Parks for factories

Over the centuries, many ways of making goods have changed. The amount of goods that can be produced from a certain area of factory floor space has gone up enormously. This means that relatively small factories can produce large amounts of goods. This explains where all the goods come from, when there appear to be so few factories.

Traditionally, people worried about making a profit and thought little about the working environment of their employees. But now, as factories earn more, this view is changing. Workers can choose which factories they want to work in and a factory in its own pleasant surroundings is as attractive to the people working in factories as it is to those working in offices.

Up to now, office-based companies have taken the lead and found pleasant settings. Now, research and development companies making high technology goods are also moving into more pleasant sites. These are often called science or industrial parks. They are the way forward for factories that produce little pollution.

(left) When factories were first built, the owners gave little thought to the expansion of their buildings. This left them cramped and trapped in the city centres.

(below) The old inner city factories are usually either demolished or made into museums or shops.

(above) The chance can be taken to make the city centre a more open place by putting parkland where factories no longer want to be. This is Teesside, in northern England, one of the birthplaces of steelmaking.

(left) This is a modern industrial park on the outskirts of Denver. People making high technology goods can work in factory environments that are not much different from offices. In the future, the difference between an office and a factory will become even more blurred.

Chapter 4

A guide to the world's industries

Our world has an amazing mix of industries, some prospering, some declining.

This continual change has happened ever since the start of the Industrial Revolution and looks set to continue. Here are some of the more important large-scale industries and the changes that they have experienced.

Industries have many names, but they all group into several basic kinds. Heavy industries are the group that make basic goods for other industries to use, or that use supplies in huge quantities. These include iron and steel, shipbuilding and part of the chemicals industry.

Medium industries are the industries of the production line, for example engineering, and making vehicles and appliances for the home.

Light industries are those in which science and skill combine to make a product out of small amounts of material. Today they are dominated by the electronics and communications industries.

❐ (left) Examining silicon sheets for imperfections before they are used to make silicon chips for the electronics industry.

❐ (right) Examining precision gear wheels before assembly.

Iron and steel

This was a leading industry of the Industrial Revolution and it is still one of the most basic industries. Iron and steel can be made on a small scale or a large scale. The early ironworks could melt and separate out (smelt) less than a tonne of iron ore. But over the last two centuries there has been a trend to smelt on a larger and larger scale. This has meant that many of the smaller furnaces have been closed down. Even important industrial countries now each have only a few giant furnaces to supply their entire needs.

> The iron and steel industry is one of the world's oldest. Because they are basic materials, many countries like to have iron and steelworks. As a result, too much steel is being produced and factories will have to be very fit to survive.

Blast furnaces work continuously day and night throughout the year. A furnace can produce 10,000 tonnes a day, the molten iron and waste rock (slag) being tapped off almost constantly.

Most ironworks produce molten iron. This can be poured into moulds and then carried by train or ship to a steelworks, where it is heated up again, melted and changed to steel. But this is very inefficient, so most steelworks are next to the iron-making plants. This means that the molten, or near molten, iron can be made into steel immediately, saving huge amounts of energy. This is why most works are combined iron and steelworks.

Steelworks

Steel is iron that has just under two percent carbon in it. Iron contains about five percent carbon, so the steelmaking process is designed to lower the amount of carbon. This is done by blowing oxygen through the molten metal.

Iron and steelworks

Iron making is one of the industries known as 'heavy industries'. Each furnace may take a charge of iron ore weighing tens of tonnes at a time. The iron ore, three quarters of which is often useless rock, has to be brought to the furnace – a very expensive exercise. There it is mixed with coke (processed coal) and some limestone. Coke, like iron, is used in very large amounts, and this, too, is very costly to transport.

In the past much more coke was used in a blast furnace than is used today. Perhaps five to six tonnes of coke were needed for each tonne of iron ore. Iron makers were therefore keen to be as close to the coal supplies as possible, and many iron and steelworks were built close to coalfields. Most of them are still located at these sites. Ironworks that are not near coal supplies nearby always import coal by ship. Therefore, these ironworks are found on the coast.

❐ (above) Inside a steel rolling mill.

Steel rolling mills   Loading docks

❑ (below) A ship collects finished steel for export.

The siting of iron and steelworks

Because ironworks need enormously large sites to store iron ore, coal, coke, limestone and waste rock from the furnace (called slag), ironworks are some of the largest industrial sites, stretching over many square kilometres. The most likely place to find such a huge space is by the coast, either on a coastal plain or on the banks of a river estuary close to the sea. This kind of site offers a flat site and a place for docks to be built alongside the works, either to bring in iron ore and coal or to take away finished iron and steel.

❑ (above) A crucible carrying molten iron to the steelworks.

❑ (above) The blast furnace

Steel furnace

Iron and coal stockpiles

Blast furnace

Some steelworks are found separately from ironworks. These are usually works that make special steels, such as stainless steel. They are often medium-sized firms which do not use much iron ore directly. Rather they use mostly scrap iron and steel. A mixture of iron and scrap is heated in an electric arc furnace, by sending enormous currents of electricity through the scrap.

Ships carry cargoes much more efficiently than in the past, so fewer ships are needed today. In addition, with less risk of global war fewer military vessels are needed. This means tough times for shipbuilders.

Once the steel has been made, it has to be shaped. Much steel is rolled into sheets; some is squeezed out to make wire.

In recent years there has been a trend to make steel mills smaller in size, so that they produce about 20-50 tonnes of steel at a time. These are called mini-mills. By having many small mills, they can be placed nearer to where scrap is collected. Mini-mills are also more easily afforded by developing countries.

The motor vehicle industry

This is the world's biggest industry. It employs about a tenth of all manufacturing workers. Except for a small market in specialist vehicles, it is an industry where only the large and powerful can survive.

Vehicle-making began in France in about 1890. Most vehicle makers had no experience at all because this was a new industry. Some companies had made bicycles, some had made horse-drawn carriages. All were attracted by the excitement and the prospect of a huge market.

The first cars were made one at a time and in small workshops. It was ten years before

Shipbuilding and repairing

Ships have been an important way in which people and goods can be carried from one part of a country to another along a coastal route, or from one country to another across an ocean.

Shipbuilding is the assembly of large water-going vessels. It is therefore essential that shipyards are either on the coast, or in sheltered river sites close to the coast. Today, shipbuilders construct modern ships that can carry over half a million tonnes of cargo. These vessels use enormous amounts of steel.

How a shipyard works

A modern shipyard (see pictures below left) assembles ships using parts, such as steel plates, that have been made elsewhere. Most shipyards have only small storage areas, so over the time that it takes to build the vessel, parts have to be delivered, either from an engineering works or direct from a steelworks. For this reason many shipbuilding yards are close to steelworks.

Once delivered, the steel plates have to be cut to their final size, bent to shape and then welded into place; all this by a large number of people.

Most of the ship is assembled in pieces, called modules. So, for example, the part of the vessel which will be the above-deck living quarters (the superstructure) may be made on shore and then lifted into place on the hull. This way the ship can be built much faster than if the superstructure had to be built after the hull.

❐ (above) If there is no space on land to build a dock, ships can be built in an estuary inside a floating dry dock like the one shown above.

❐ (below, left and far left) The people working in this shipyard in New Orleans (USA) are dwarfed by the huge size of the ship they are building. Shipyards have little flexibility in where they can be sited. In New Orleans, the giant Mississippi River gives flat land, a navigable channel and a sheltered site not too far from the sea.

vehicles were made in factories in the United States, and to begin with the quality of cars made there was well below that of cars made in Europe.

The big difference between the European and United States vehicle-builders was that the Europeans built all the parts they needed themselves, whereas in the United States vehicles were assembled using parts they bought in from other firms.

But whichever way firms chose to build, it was soon clear that this was a business that had to be organised on a big scale, so from the thousands of small firms that tried their hand at making vehicles in the 1890s, there were only about 50 by 1930.

> The chemicals industry works with liquids and gases, producing huge volumes of materials by processes that run all the time. A great deal of money is needed to build such plants, but relatively few people are needed to work in them.

The main reason the United States became the leader of vehicle-making was largely due to Henry Ford. He founded the Ford Motor Company in 1903, and in 1908 he invented the famous Model T, the first mass-produced car in the world. It used the revolutionary idea of an assembly line using standard, mass-produced parts. It was an immediate success.

In 1908 the General Motors Corporation was founded by William Durant. Durant had the idea of producing a range of cars that were basically the same, but which allowed people to have a small choice in the kind of car they would buy.

By coincidence, both Ford and General Motors were founded in Detroit. Thus, as the two companies prospered, Detroit grew up as the world's motor vehicle centre.

The chemicals industry

The chemicals industry uses natural materials to make a wide range of chemicals such as petroleum for our cars, fertilisers for farms, medicines, plastics, detergents and so on. The chemicals industry relies on research for its success. Everything from the carbon in resistors to the silicon in chips is a result of the chemicals industry's research.

The chemicals industry has grown enormously in the 20th century because researchers have found ways to recombine molecules to make completely new substances. About a thousand new substances are put on the market each year. At the same time it has been organised to make large volumes of materials automatically. So while the products from the chemicals industry have grown, the numbers working in the industry have shrunk.

The chemicals industry uses a wide range of raw materials, most of which have to be delivered to the factory in bulk. Liquids, such as crude oil, can come by pipeline directly from the oil well, or they can arrive by ship. Chemicals based on petroleum are called organic. From them come refined petroleum, synthetic fibres and plastics.

Materials that come in solid form usually arrive by ship or train. These can include limestone, salt rock and other basic materials quarried from the ground. The chemicals based on rocks, water and gases in the air are called inorganic chemicals. Products include soaps, bleaches, table salt, paints and explosives.

Most countries have their own chemicals companies, but the largest are in the USA, Japan and Europe, because these places have the biggest markets. Japan is unusual because it has so very few raw materials and virtually everything has to be imported. For this reason it makes only specialised chemicals that have a high value when they are sold.

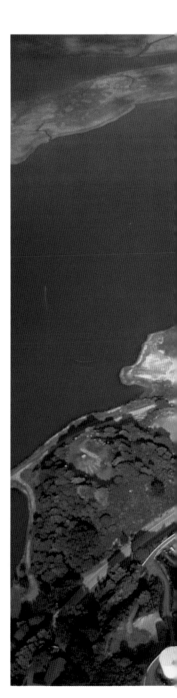

❐ (right) Chemical works require a huge area of flat land, as pipes carry the various by-products and products from one process to another to make the best use of the energy.

The size of chemical plants

Many of the processes that make chemicals only work with very expensive equipment that can produce high temperatures and pressures. Much of the process also happens when the chemicals are liquids. This combination tends to work best when factories are very large, and when they make chemicals continuously with many automated processes.

This is why a chemical factory looks like a mass of vessels connected by pipes, and why so few people are seen around them.

❐ (right) Power stations are needed on site to generate the energy for running chemical plants.

❐ (below) A major product of the chemicals industry is plastics. Here plastic bottles are being examined for quality.

The United States is a large country, and for a long time it was not served by a dense network of railways. As a result, many people wanted a car. By contrast, fewer European people saw a need for the car. So, while European makers could only sell cars by the thousand, in the United States cars sold by the million. European manufacturers soon only built for the wealthy; manufacturers in the United States built for everyone.

> Motor car factories now tend to build just one model. As a result, showrooms may be stocked with cars bearing the same maker's name, but which are produced in many different countries.

The motor vehicle industry soon became a huge consumer of iron and steel as well as rubber (for tyres), glass (for windscreens) and petroleum (as fuel). In this way the motor industry caused the growth of many other industries as well.

Companies in the United States first began to use their success to open factories in other parts of the world, beginning in Europe. Ford began its own European companies, while General Motors bought out established European companies (Vauxhall in Britain, Opel in Germany, Holden in Australia).

After World War 2 the motor vehicle industry began to change. There was a much stronger demand in Europe and Japan, and in each country motor companies began to grow quickly (Volkswagen, Renault, Fiat and Rover in Europe; Toyota, Nissan and Honda in Japan).

European and Japanese cars were smaller and used less fuel. They also began to be built with a different styling, and more importantly, they began to get very much more reliable. This meant that the United States gradually lost its lead. In 1950 the United States produced two-thirds of the world's motor vehicles; in the

Modern automobile making

Motor cars are some of the most complicated things made in a factory in large numbers. To make them efficiently most makers use a system called production line working. You can see it in the pictures on this page.

The key to production line working is that a motorised conveyor carries the car frame very slowly across the assembly hall. Along the line groups of workers are responsible for fitting and checking parts of the assembly.

Manufacturers begin with a standard body, and then add a variety of bolt-on modifications. Thus, they can produce a variety of cars to suit different customer tastes.

❏ (below) Engines are made from solid blocks of steel or aluminium and have to be machined carefully to the correct shapes.

❏ (below) The main car production line in detail.

❏ (left) Engines, the most complex part of the car, are made separately from the body and added near the end of the assembly line. This is the final stage of engine assembly. Notice how the assembly hall is clean and spacious

❏ (below) Many of the tasks for assembly are done by robots because they give a more even result and better reliability. The robots here are welding parts of the car body.

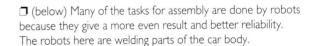

❏ (above) Dip-painting the body.

❏ (right) The lower frame, engine and body panels all come together in the final stages of assembly.

early 1990s it produced less than a fifth. Most of the cars in the world are produced by the Japanese.

The greatest density of cars are in North America, Western Europe, Japan, Australia, and New Zealand, each of which has about one car for every two or three people. But there is huge scope for more growth. For example, in China at present there is only one car for every two thousand people.

Passenger aircraft

The aircraft industry has been one of the success stories of this century. From making just a few small planes, it has become one of the world's leading industries. There are two branches: one makes passenger aircraft, and the other makes military aircraft and space equipment.

> The aircraft industry is expected to expand fast, as more and more people want to fly between countries. But making aircraft is so expensive that nearly all of them are made by just a few giant companies.

The one single development that helped the aircraft industry to succeed was the invention of the jet engine about 50 years ago. This allowed aircraft to fly faster, to be more powerful, and so to carry

Aerospace

Motor vehicles began life just a few years before aircraft, and both have become centres of high technology. But whereas motor vehicles are made by the million, aircraft, and especially space craft, are produced one at a time. It is said that a jumbo jet is the most complex machine ever made.

The aerospace industry makes incredibly complex machines that cost huge sums of money. In general, like the motor vehicle industry, it has just a few giant players. It is dominated by those such as Boeing and McDonnell Douglas in the USA, European companies such as British Aerospace, and Russian companies.

But these manufacturers are really planners and assemblers. They do not make all the hundreds of thousands of parts they need. Instead, these are made by thousands of small engineering companies, often working on a small scale, to high levels of precision, in workshops rather than in factories.

The aerospace industry is made of two main parts: the airframe makers such as Boeing, and the engine makers such as Rolls-Royce and General Electric. When an airline buys, for example, a jumbo jet, it first buys an airframe, then it selects which company will supply the engines.

This page gives you a view of how an advanced engine-builder works. Only a few engines are made each year, but each must be built to the highest standards and run reliably and safely for millions of kilometres. This puts great pressure on the skills of engineers and manufacturers who make the parts used by engine-builders.

❏ (above) Engines and airframes come together to make a jumbo jet.

❏ (right and far right) Engineers testing an aircraft engine.

❏ (left) The aircraft engine equivalent of the production line. Here, several huge engines are suspended so that they can be worked on by the production teams.

more people more reliably for longer distances.

As with motor vehicles, the vast distances between places in the United States created a demand for aircraft and made United States companies early leaders in the race to be world-class aircraft-makers. But many countries wanted to have a hand in aircraft development because they needed fighter planes for their defence, so the industry developed both in Europe and America.

Since World War 2, there has been intense competition, not only to build aircraft, but also space equipment such as rockets and satellites. Many countries have been involved in this effort.

The aircraft industry uses the most advanced techniques and scientific ideas, so it produces many ideas which can be used to make goods for everyday use. For example, the satellites that now link part of the world's telephone systems were first developed for military use, in the form of tracking satellites and space craft.

The electronics industry

The electronics industry has grown up with the developments in electricity and materials. It is entirely a research-based industry, even though its products are now found in every walk of life. The electronics industry, more than perhaps any other, is made of companies that operate on a worldwide basis so that they can provide the latest in technology at the lowest price.

Electronics will dominate our future. New 'information superhighways' are already being built across America and Europe.

The electronics industry began with explorations in radio and communications. Thomas Edison discovered the principle of the electronic valve when he was working with electric lamps

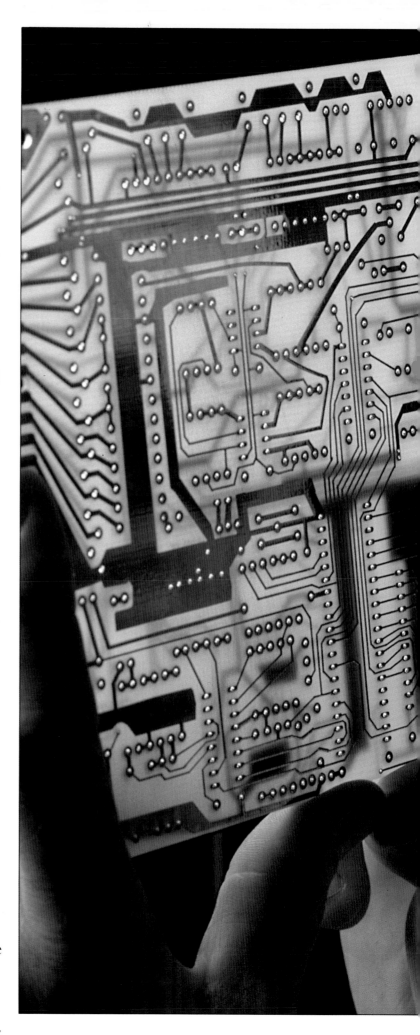

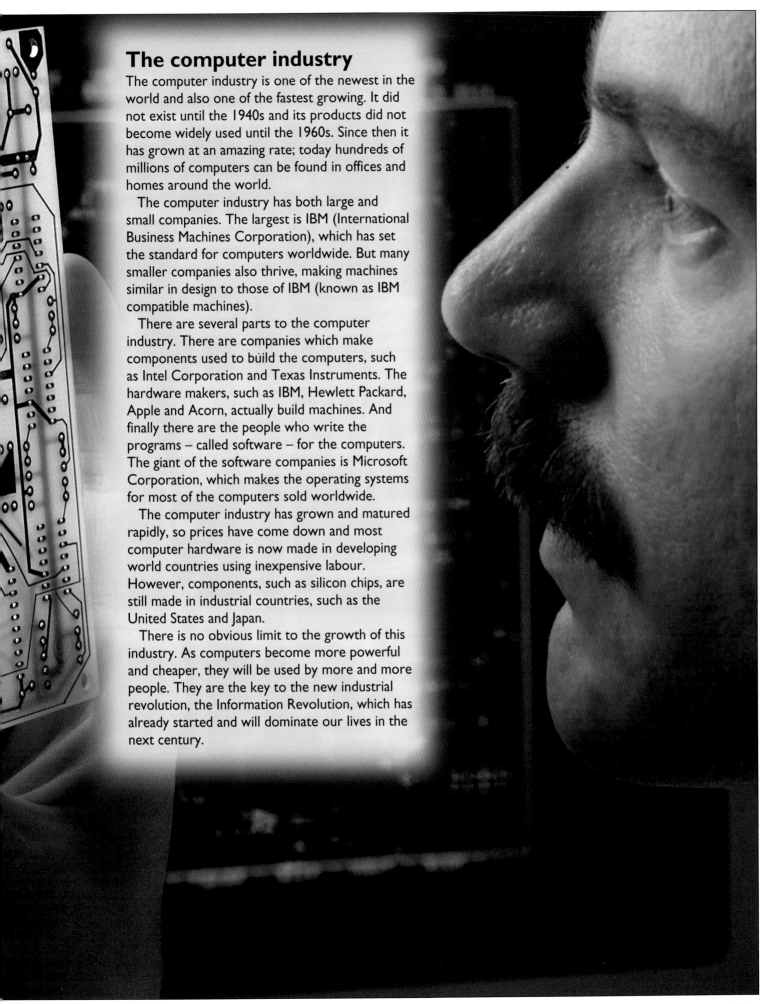

The computer industry

The computer industry is one of the newest in the world and also one of the fastest growing. It did not exist until the 1940s and its products did not become widely used until the 1960s. Since then it has grown at an amazing rate; today hundreds of millions of computers can be found in offices and homes around the world.

The computer industry has both large and small companies. The largest is IBM (International Business Machines Corporation), which has set the standard for computers worldwide. But many smaller companies also thrive, making machines similar in design to those of IBM (known as IBM compatible machines).

There are several parts to the computer industry. There are companies which make components used to build the computers, such as Intel Corporation and Texas Instruments. The hardware makers, such as IBM, Hewlett Packard, Apple and Acorn, actually build machines. And finally there are the people who write the programs – called software – for the computers. The giant of the software companies is Microsoft Corporation, which makes the operating systems for most of the computers sold worldwide.

The computer industry has grown and matured rapidly, so prices have come down and most computer hardware is now made in developing world countries using inexpensive labour. However, components, such as silicon chips, are still made in industrial countries, such as the United States and Japan.

There is no obvious limit to the growth of this industry. As computers become more powerful and cheaper, they will be used by more and more people. They are the key to the new industrial revolution, the Information Revolution, which has already started and will dominate our lives in the next century.

towards the end of the 19th century. At the turn of the century, Luigi Marconi made the first radio broadcast. It was all done on a small scale by a group of dedicated scientists.

But it did not take long for other manufacturers and for governments to see the importance of the work that was being done. This was the world's first important industry, where the value of the product – radio, television, computer – was very high compared to the value of the materials. It did not use huge assembly lines like the motor car industry and it did not need vast amounts of raw materials like chemicals.

> The textile industry shows how cheap labour can cut costs even more effectively than high-speed machinery. But this is not good news for the workers in developing countries who must accept low wages.

The electronics industry was not tied down to its sources of raw materials like the other industries. It did not need a large factory or a flat site; it did not even need good road and rail links. It simply needed very clever research and development, and this could occur anywhere. As a result, the electronics industry has found it very easy to move about and relocate, and has been called 'footloose'.

Consumer electronics

Electronics have changed people's lives. Many things that were once done by mechanical means are now done faster and more reliably by electronics. This has caused many traditional firms to go out of business and has provided the opportunity for other industries to rise up to become world giants.

A good example of the change that has occurred has been the watch industry.

The textile industry

The textile industry makes cloth from fibres and is probably the oldest industry in the world. Although textiles are often made on the most advanced machinery, they are quite easily made on a hand loom. This allowed the textile industry to be the first to grow at the start of the Industrial Revolution. It soon became the most important industry in England, and as it grew demanded new machines, which in turn caused a growth in the engineering industry.

Ironically, the same advantages that allowed textiles to lead the Industrial Revolution make it extremely hard for the industry to survive in the modern industrial world. Just as

❒ (below) An Indian housewife in a rural village spins on a simple frame in her back room. Millions like her represent a vast, though largely unseen, source of textiles in the developing world. It is the simplicity of textile-making that allowed the first Industrial Revolution to begin, and still allows people with little money to become involved in industry.

England did two centuries ago, the countries of the developing world can use their skilled workers to make textiles on simple, low-cost machines or even on hand frames. By paying workers low wages, many developing countries can make cloth at a lower cost than the giant industrial companies fitted with the fastest and most modern machines.

This challenge has caused the industry to change greatly (see 'Ever-moving business', page 14). Industrial countries are less able to make textiles using natural fibres such as cotton (as raw materials have to be imported from developing countries) but they are still able to make synthetic (artificial) fibres using oil-based materials from local chemical works.

Because making clothes can also be done in developing world countries using low-cost labour, mass-produced garments tend to be made in the developing world. Industrial countries now concentrate mostly on fashion goods; these change from month to month and it is hard for developing countries to match the constant change in demand.

❏ (below) A modern synthetic fibre being wound on to giant bobbins in a factory.

Almost half the world's watches were, at one time, made in Switzerland, a country renowned for its precision engineers. But the invention of the digital watch changed all this. Digital watches don't not need the skills of a mechanical watch engineer. This meant that this kind of watch could be assembled in low-skill areas of the developing world and sold far more cheaply. Thus, the price of watches tumbled and the watch industry moved from Switzerland to East Asia.

Construction is the world's largest industry, but it is so familiar we tend not even to notice it is there!

The watch is an example of consumer electronics. But the nature of electronics has provided almost endless opportunities from televisions and radios, computers and games machines, to camcorders, video players and personal CD players.

Japan has been in the forefront of this revolution. Most of the world's largest electronics companies are in Japan, although the technology used was invented and developed in Europe and North America. This is partly because the Japanese have put huge amounts of resources into the consumer electronics field, but also because they have been supported by their government more than Europe or North America.

Industrial and military electronics

The electronics goods we see in high street stores make up only part of the electronics revolution: the mass market end with huge numbers of appliances using simple electronics. But there is another side to the electronics industry, involving very high levels of research and development, needed, for example, to send communications satellites into space or to launch guided missiles in times of conflict.

The construction industry

The building – or construction – industry, builds the world's factories, offices, homes, roads and other structures. It is unusual among major industries in that even the largest companies do not work in large factories. Construction companies do nearly all their work on their customer's sites, where the buildings are being constructed.

Most large buildings now have a steel frame, with walls and floors of concrete. Most homes are built of brick, with a timber frame. Roads use concrete, rock rubble and tarmac.

All building activity uses a large amount of raw materials, many of which have a low value and must be obtained locally. For example, the gravel to make concrete is nearly always found from sites within thirty to fifty kilometres of the building.

The building industry is made of two quite separate sizes of firm. The majority of builders are small companies, which mainly build homes, a few at a time. The skills needed for this kind of construction are simple and no complex equipment is needed. Most home-builders therefore work in their own local area.

By contrast, the construction companies that build office towers or major highways employ tens of thousands of people and often build overseas as well as in their own country. They use heavy moving equipment, specialised machines and teams of specialist engineers.

(left) Construction sites require massive amounts of materials as well as large machines to handle them. Building sites are so familiar that we may not stop to think how much money is actually involved in each project.

(right) The construction industry is not just involved in building houses and offices; a major part of the industry builds roads, dams and similar projects.

(below) The construction industry, allied with the skills of architects, is responsible for all of the world's built environment, something that we may easily take for granted.

Prefabricated parts

Prefabricated parts are made up before being taken to the site. For example, the wall panels for large offices may be prefabricated in a factory, moved to the building site and then hung on the steel frame. This means that the building can be put up more quickly and more cheaply by making many similar units at the same time.

At present, these industries are dominated by companies in Europe and North America. However, Japan may well become a leader in this field too. Japan already has more robots than any other country in the world, and it is beginning to launch its own satellites. Its government has now begun a program that will lead to enormous investments in the new information revolution which has just started.

Industries of the future

In the last century, when machines driven by machines were still a new invention, the industries of today would have seemed to be impossible. After all, the materials and technologies used by today's industries had not even been dreamt of! Now we are used to the white hot pace of invention and discovery.

The future will bring many changes: in communication, in how goods are manufactured, and above all in the developing world.

We can expect the next change in industry to be concerned with communications. Computers are already part of many people's lives, and as computers become more powerful, we will have more and more information at our fingertips. Industries like telephone companies will grow quickly, as they can provide information through cables that will connect homes to shops and factories around the world.

We also know that the days when everyone was prepared to buy the same mass-produced article are over. Now people want their goods to be more varied, and industries are scaling down to make this possible.

Perhaps the most startling change may come from countries that at present are called the developing world. The developments of the mid-20th century which changed everybody's lives in the industrial world, had quite a small impact on the developing world. However, today many countries of Asia, including Malaysia, Singapore, Taiwan and Korea, have already begun to be called newly industrialised countries. The vast bulk of the world's people, in China and India, have not yet become part of the industrial world, although there is every sign that China will take over as the world centre of manufacturing within the next 20 years. It is less clear when India will be able to follow.

What is also clear is that the world will continue to grow, so the amount of goods that people will need will continue to rise. This is good news, because it means that many people will need to be employed to meet the demand, but the same demand will also put severe strains on the world's environment, as more resources and energy are used up. What is certain, however, is that half a century from now the world will be a very different place to that we see around us today, and most of the change will have been brought about by the people who work in the world's factories.

Glossary

DEVELOPING WORLD

Countries where the majority of people still depend on farming for their living, where wages are poor and there is a lack of advanced technology such as electricity. There are 125 countries classified by the United Nations as coming into this category, including most of those in Asia, Africa and South America.

FACTORIES

A factory is normally thought of as a special building designed for the large-scale manufacturing of goods. Factories do not have to be involved in mass-production, although some, like bottle-making or motor car-making, have production lines.

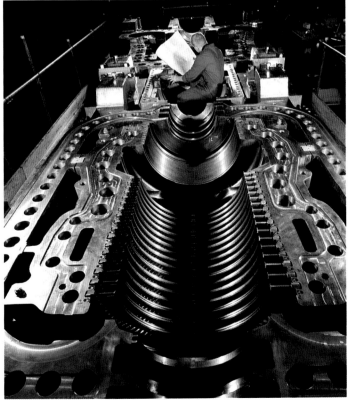

INDUSTRIAL REVOLUTION

The time during the 18th and 19th centuries when the world first saw automatic machines and steam power. Its most common symbol was the factory.

MANUFACTURING INDUSTRY

Manufacturers take simple materials and, using their skills and machines, make complicated goods. The word manufacturing can be used for any maker of goods. Half a century ago more people worked in manufacturing than in any other form of work. Since that time machines and automation have allowed a single worker to make as many goods as it took many workers before. As a result the number of people in manufacturing, especially in the industrial world, has gone down, and rarely accounts for more than three people in ten today.

RAW MATERIALS

Supplies for industry that have not been processed in any way. They might include petroleum, or cotton harvested from fields. An engineering factory might regard sheets of steel as a raw material because the steel is the material they work with; it has not been processed or altered in any way.

WORKSHOPS

Workshops are places designed for making goods, but they are smaller than factories. There is no easy way to separate out a workshop from a factory, except that, in a factory, there are managers whose task is to manage the flow of work in an organised way. In a workshop the relations between workers and owner is usually much less obvious, and all do a range of similar tasks.

Further reading

This book is one of a series that covers the whole of geography. They may provide you with more information. The series is:

1. **People** of the world, population & migration
2. **Homes** of the world & the way people live
3. The world's **shops** & where they are
4. **Cities** of the world & their future
5. World **transport**, travel & communications
6. **Farms** & the world's food supply

7. World **industry** & making goods
8. The world's **resources** & their exploitation
9. The world's changing **energy** supplies
10. The world's **environments** & conservation
11. World **weather**, climate & climatic change
12. The **Earth** & its changing surface

Index

aerospace industry 54
aircraft 54
aircraft industry 14, 54
alloys 30
Asia 24, 34, 62
assembly line 31, 50, 51
Australasia 32
automation 32
automobile 8, 10, 52
automobile making 52

BASF 30
blast furnace 22, 24, 28, 46, 47
Boeing 54
Britain 30
British Aerospace 54
business parks 42

canal 26, 28
change 10
chemicals industry 8, 14, 45, 50
China 19, 22, 23, 34, 62
city 27, 40
city centres 16
clocks 24
coal 24, 26, 27, 28, 38, 47
coal mining 28
coal field 27, 28, 38
communications 45, 56
computer industry 57
Computer Integrated Manufacturing 32
computers 8, 32, 62
construction industry 60
consumer electronics 58, 60
crafts 8, 12
craftspeople 22
cutlery 14

Darby, Abraham 24
developing world 5, 8, 40, 58, 62, 63
discoveries 30

East Asia 10, 34
East Europe 17
Edison, Thomas 56

electricity 30
electronics industry 14, 45, 56, 60
energy 13, 38
engineering 22, 28, 45
engineering industry 28, 30
environment 16, 17
Europe 10, 22, 24, 32, 50, 60

factories 6, 8, 12, 14, 24, 25, 26, 30, 37, 63
family businesses 10
fashion goods 58
finished goods 12
firearms 23
flatted-factory 31
footloose 58
Ford, Henry 30, 50
France 30

General Electric Company 54
General Motors Corporation 50
Germany 30
goods 5, 8
Great Britain 20
gunsmith 23

Halifax 6
handicrafts 10
handwork 12
handworking 12
heavy industries 45
high technology 12
household system 9

IBM 57
India 19, 22, 62
industrial cities 37
industrial estates 6, 40
industrial landscape 24
industrial parks 42
Industrial Revolution 20, 24, 46, 58, 63
industrial world 8, 32
industry 8
Information Revolution 57
inorganic chemicals 50
inventions 19, 20, 22
Iron Age 20

iron and steel industry 14, 28, 45, 46, 47
iron and steelworks 46
ironworks 46
Islamic countries 22

Japan 19, 32, 34, 52, 57, 60
jewellery industry 10

Kenya 9
Korea 19, 62

laboratory 34
light industries 45

machines 8, 20, 24
machine tools 28
Malaysia 62
managers 26
manufacturers 7, 12
manufacturing 12
manufacturing industry 5, 63
manufacturing system 12
Marconi, Luigi 58
market 38
mass production 14, 30, 32
materials 30, 38, 63
medium industries 45
metal working 20
Middle East 19
military electronics 60
motor vehicle industry 48, 52

North America 10, 24, 32, 60

office work 7
organic chemicals 30

people 34, 35, 40
Philippines 11
pipeline 50
planners 16, 42
plastics 30, 50
pollution 17
pottery 5
processing 13
production line 30, 45, 52

radio 32
railway 26, 28, 29

railway industry 28
raw materials 12, 17, 40, 50, 58, 60, 63
Research and development 34
robots 19, 32, 62
Rolls-Royce 19, 54

Savery, Thomas 28
science 22, 30
science parks 42
shipbuilding 45
ships 22
shipyards 48
shop floor 34
silicon chip 8
Singapore 62
site 38
skill 8, 12
skilled work 10
skilled workers 33
small businesses 10, 42
software 57
steam engine 24, 28
steam power 26
steelworks 5, 46, 48
Stone Age 20
suburbs 42
Switzerland 60
synthetic fibres 50

Taiwan 62
technology 8, 22, 23
telephone companies 62
television 32
textile industry 14, 26, 58
textile mill 27
tools 20
trade 22
transport 28

unemployment 16
United States 30, 50, 57
unskilled people 33

wages 8
water power 26
water wheel 28
Watt, James 28
wealth 6
weapons 20, 28
workers 6
workshops 10, 12, 14, 63

World Geography People of the world, population & migration Homes of the world & the way people live The world's shops & where they are Cities of the world &
changing energy supplies The world's environment & conservation World weather, climate & climatic change The Earth & its changing surface World Geography
travel & communications Farms & the world's food supply World industry & making goods The world's resources & their exploitation The world's changing energy st
& migration Homes of the world & the way people live The world's shops & where they are Cities of the world & their future World transport, travel & communicatio
& conservation World weather, climate & climatic change The Earth & its changing surface World Geography People of the world, population & migration Home
supply World industry & making goods The world's resources & their exploitation The world's changing energy supplies The world's environment & conservation V
live The world's shops & where they are Cities of the world & their future World transport, travel & communications Farms & the world's food supply World indus
change The Earth & its changing surface World Geography People of the world, population & migration Homes of the world & the way people live The world's sho
resources & their exploitation The world's changing energy supplies The world's environment & conservation World weather, climate & climatic change The Earth
of the world & their future World transport, travel & communications Farms & the world's food supply World industry & making goods The world's resources & thei
Geography People of the world, population & migration Homes of the world & the way people live The world's shops & where they are Cities of the world & their fut
energy supplies The world's environment & conservation World weather, climate & climatic change The Earth & its changing surface World Geography People o
communications Farms & the world's food supply World industry & making goods The world's resources & their exploitation The world's changing energy supplies Th
Homes of the world & the way people live The world's shops & where they are Cities of the world & their future World transport, travel & communications Farms &
World weather, climate & climatic change The Earth & its changing surface World Geography People of the world, population & migration Homes of the world &
industry & making goods The world's resources & their exploitation The world's changing energy supplies The world's environment & conservation World weathe
world's shops & where they are Cities of the world & their future World transport, travel & communications Farms & the world's food supply World industry & m
The Earth & its changing surface World Geography People of the world, population & migration Homes of the world & the way people live The world's shops & wh
& their exploitation The world's changing energy supplies The world's environment & conservation World weather, climate & climatic change The Earth & its chan
& their future World transport, travel & communications Farms & the world's food supply World industry & making goods The world's resources & their exploitation
People of the world, population & migration Homes of the world & the way people live The world's shops & where they are Cities of the world & their future Worla
supplies The world's environment & conservation World weather, climate & climatic change The Earth & its changing surface World Geography People of the world,
Farms & the world's food supply World industry & making goods The world's resources & their exploitation The world's changing energy supplies The world's env
of the world & the way people live The world's shops & where they are Cities of the world & their future World transport, travel & communications Farms & the worl
weather, climate & climatic change The Earth & its changing surface World Geography People of the world, population & migration Homes of the world & the wa
& making goods The world's resources & their exploitation The world's changing energy supplies The world's environment & conservation World weather, climate &
& where they are Cities of the world & their future World transport, travel & communications Farms & the world's food supply World industry & making goods 1
& its changing surface World Geography People of the world, population & migration Homes of the world & the way people live The world's shops & where they ar
exploitation The world's changing energy supplies The world's environment & conservation World weather, climate & climatic change The Earth & its changing sur
future World transport, travel & communications Farms & the world's food supply World industry & making goods The world's resources & their exploitation The u
of the world, population & migration Homes of the world & the way people live The world's shops & where they are Cities of the world & their future World transpe
The world's environment & conservation World weather, climate & climatic change The Earth & its changing surface World Geography People of the world, popi
Farms & the world's food supply World industry & making goods The world's resources & their exploitation The world's changing energy supplies The world's env
of the world & the way people live The world's shops & where they are Cities of the world & their future World transport, travel & communications Farms & the worl
weather, climate & climatic change The Earth & its changing surface World Geography People of the world, population & migration Homes of the world & the wa
& making goods The world's resources & their exploitation The world's changing energy supplies The world's environment & conservation World weather, climate &
& where they are Cities of the world & their future World transport, travel & communications Farms & the world's food supply World industry & making goods 1
& its changing surface World Geography People of the world, population & migration Homes of the world & the way people live The world's shops & where they ar
exploitation The world's changing energy supplies The world's environment & conservation World weather, climate & climatic change The Earth & its changing sur
future World transport, travel & communications Farms & the world's food supply World industry & making goods The world's resources & their exploitation The u
of the world, population & migration Homes of the world & the way people live The world's shops & where they are Cities of the world & their future World transpe
The world's environment & conservation World weather, climate & climatic change The Earth & its changing surface World Geography People of the world, popi
Farms & the world's food supply World industry & making goods The world's resources & their exploitation The world's changing energy supplies The world's env
of the world & the way people live The world's shops & where they are Cities of the world & their future World transport, travel & communications Farms & the worl
weather, climate & climatic change The Earth & its changing surface World Geography People of the world, population & migration Homes of the world & the wa
& making goods The world's resources & their exploitation The world's changing energy supplies The world's environment & conservation World weather, climate &
& where they are Cities of the world & their future World transport, travel & communications Farms & the world's food supply World industry & making goods
& its changing surface World Geography People of the world, population & migration Homes of the world & the way people live The world's shops & where they ar
exploitation The world's changing energy supplies The world's environment & conservation World weather, climate & climatic change The Earth & its changing sur
future World transport, travel & communications Farms & the world's food supply World industry & making goods The world's resources & their exploitation The u
of the world, population & migration Homes of the world & the way people live The world's shops & where they are Cities of the world & their future World transp
The world's environment & conservation World weather, climate & climatic change The Earth & its changing surface World Geography People of the world, popi
Farms & the world's food supply World industry & making goods The world's resources & their exploitation The world's changing energy supplies The world's env
of the world & the way people live The world's shops & where they are Cities of the world & their future World transport, travel & communications Farms & the worl
weather, climate & climatic change The Earth & its changing surface World Geography People of the world, population & migration Homes of the world & the wa
& making goods The world's resources & their exploitation The world's changing energy supplies The world's environment & conservation World weather, climate &
& where they are Cities of the world & their future World transport, travel & communications Farms & the world's food supply World industry & making goods
& its changing surface World Geography People of the world, population & migration Homes of the world & the way people live The world's shops & where they
exploitation The world's changing energy supplies The world's environment & conservation World weather, climate & climatic change The Earth & its changing sui
future World transport, travel & communications Farms & the world's food supply World industry & making goods The world's resources & their exploitation
of the world & the way people live The world's shops & where they are Cities of the world & their future World transport, travel & communications Farms & the
weather, climate & climatic change The Earth & its changing surface World Geography People of the world, population & migration Homes of the world & the wa
& making goods The world's resources & their exploitation The world's changing energy supplies The world's environment & conservation World weather, climate &
& where they are Cities of the world & their future World transport, travel & communications Farms & the world's food supply World industry & making goods
& its changing surface World Geography People of the world, population & migration Homes of the world & the way people live The world's shops & where they
exploitation The world's changing energy supplies The world's environment & conservation World weather, climate & climatic change The Earth & its changing su
future World transport, travel & communications Farms & the world's food supply World industry & making goods The world's resources & their exploitation